ROBERT E. LEE'S ORDERLY

A MODERN BLACK MAN'S CONFEDERATE JOURNEY

BY AL ARNOLD

Contents

This Corner Stone,
this solid ground,
firm through the
fiercest drought
& Storm!
In Him!
Al____
5/31/10

FOREWORD

In the interest of full disclosure, Al Arnold is a dear brother in Christ, fellow church member, respected Elder, friend, and we both share a deep love of history. We have often discussed history over fellowship meals at our church in Jackson, MS. To say that I was surprised one night when I was talking with him and he was speaking about the Confederate war effort with a positive, almost glowing, affection would be to put it mildly. I was shocked. I had never met an African-American male in the South who celebrated both his Confederate heritage and admiration for the battle tactics, leadership skills and principles of Confederate generals. I was speechless.

I grew up in Charleston, South Carolina, the descendent of Caucasian ancestors who fought for the Confederacy on every side of my family. We even have family who participated in the American Revolution. This is a deep, deep point of pride to my family, which we often discussed, documented and displayed to others via pictures and family papers throughout our home. There was also an appreciation for these ancestors, especially their honor in service to their country, and I grew up around and sharing in that sentiment. However, as my formal training as a historian began, I learned about some of the reasons why my ancestors and other White Southerners fought. They were fighting, in many ways, to maintain a system of inhuman bondage that was meant to protect a "for-profit" enterprise fraught with man stealing, abuse and mistreatment of other human beings for their own economic gain in what historians have called "the peculiar institution," otherwise known as the institution of slavery. There is no way around this, and no serious historian can deny that slavery is the major reason why the Civil War was fought. Similar to Arnold's path, this is a personal journey I had to go on, come to grips with, process, lament and I have tried to use this truth in order to teach, repent and bring healing, unity as well as reconciliation among African Americans and Whites in my beloved South.

To be sure, I can sympathize with Arnold not only in my personal journey in understanding race in the South as a descendent of Confederate ancestry, but also in my journey through research as a historian and scholar. My own research focuses on White missionaries to enslaved Africans through "slave mission" churches in the antebellum South. I argue that through these churches a measure of ecclesiastical equality as well as education, dignity and honor was afforded to some enslaved individuals through church membership in the midst of a dehumanizing institution that seldom recognized one's humanity. Some scholars have said that since the missionaries I am studying are operating within a paternalistic system built on slavery, then the impetus for their motivations had to be driven by a racist social order that could only be interested in buttressing and supporting dehumanization of the African through slavery. Therefore, to them, slave missions could not in any way be "life giving," freeing or beneficial to the lives of the enslaved, but only damaging and controlling. However, I genuinely deal with the faith, theology and motivations of these missionaries whom I sense possessed a deep love, respect and care for enslaved Africans. They often genuinely seemed to care about the souls of enslaved Africans and even brought some measure of temporal freedoms to the lives of their church members. This adds complexity, nuance and balance to our understanding of the institution of slavery and to the multiethnic religious life of the South. Sometimes we find White Southerners who are functioning in this system and attempted to undo the effects of slavery in ways that were quite countercultural. For instance, one of the missionaries I study used to record the first and surname of enslaved Africans in the church record books. This displayed that the missionary thought of the enslaved members as human, with lineages and with ancestry. It was a subtle display of resistance to the status quo, which seldom ever recorded an enslaved African's surname or would have ever even suggested that he possessed one. Just as it is both myopic and false to say that all African Americans only supported the Union effort, it would also be shortsighted and limiting to assume that all White Southerners were racists, only wanted to dehumanize enslaved Africans and, as Christians, never questioned for themselves the implications of the institution of slavery.

I also grew up around many African Americans who were friends, fellow church members and brothers and sisters in Christ. These individuals often expressed deep pain over symbols such as the Confederate flag because to them it had come to represent hate, White supremacy and segregation. It was used as a symbol to maintain Jim Crow, to oppose the Civil Rights movement and was the symbol under which the soldiers of the Confederate States of America fought to maintain their "way of life" (which was largely based on an agrarian economy that could not function without the institution of slavery). I have therefore come to the conclusion that I will not choose to celebrate my Confederate heritage through the display of Confederate symbols.

I personally came to this conclusion because I do not wish to continue to hurt or offend my African-American brothers and sisters more than that which has already been created by three hundred years of enslavement and a hundred years more of being treated as second-class citizens. Instead, I have chosen to use my ancestry (I don't hide my Confederate ancestry. I am always very clear about where I come from.) to teach students about our nation's history and how sometimes people made decisions (like treating human beings as chattel property and like animals) and became blinded by greed, culture and the pursuit of mammon. I deeply believe that if my ancestors are in heaven right now that they would not want me to continue to display a prideful heritage that largely divides us as a people. They would, rather, want their memories and lives to be used to unite people across all racial lines, in love of one another and in Christ. My calling is first and foremost that of a Christian. This citizenship trumps all other citizenships and heritages. The cross of Christ is more important to me than my Southern heritage and deeply more important than a Confederate flag. My conclusion then is that my service to Christ, who would have me lay down all things that might be a stumbling block to love and fellowship with others, is more important than my devotion to a nationalistic or Confederate symbol. I am, therefore, willing to lay down those things for the sake of the gospel and for loving my brother and sister and to not cause them more pain.

As I have grown in my understanding of history through graduate study and teaching history courses over the past decade at universities across the South, I have realized one thing: history is complex. There are no easy ways to process it, teach it, research it and explain it. It is as complex and nuanced as there are people that one is trying to understand. Each person possesses different views, different agendas, different ideals and principles. To generalize and say "all African Americans detested the Confederacy and supported the Union cause" sounds good, is politically correct, is what I wish were true, but it is not totally true nor is it faithful to the complexity of the U.S. South, the history of the United States nor of humanity. Now, historians have come to accept that the overwhelming majority of African Americans supported the Union cause and would have chosen freedom over continued enslavement. That much is abundantly clear. However, what then do we do with men like Turner Hall, Jr.? How do we as historians interpret enslaved African Americans who picked up weapons and fought bravely for a Confederate cause and for a master whom they respected and loved? How do we make sense of an African-American man who would later, in 1938, in the very midst of a country that celebrated segregation as "separate but equal," attend a Confederate Veterans reunion as an honored guest?

Many historians would say that there are power dynamics in play that kept Turner Hall, Jr. from expressing his true feelings. Perhaps he was fearful of what would happen to him if he did not support his master. After all, three centuries of brutal suppression of one's humanity, dignity and autonomy would have conditioned people to submit, right? However, I do not believe this is the full story. I do not believe this because Turner Hall, Jr. had dignity, agency, and choice. That choice needs to be respected. I also believe this because of the powerful presentation of Al Arnold's journey. I am forced, as a historian, to admit that perhaps the story is more complex than power dynamics, race, economics, gender and institutions. Perhaps Hall really did have feelings of love and admiration for the South. Perhaps he had similar sentiments for his master and really did believe in the Confederate War effort, so much so that he would give his own life. Who am I as a historian to neglect or abandon this historical figure's belief simply because it does not conform to the overwhelming narrative? Perhaps there were others who believed this way and their stories need to be made known as well.

Furthermore, historians need to continue to probe and examine, as well as interpret, the impact that African Americans played in the Confederate war effort as servants, orderlies, spies, trench diggers, cooks, body servants and even as soldiers. This is not to mention the millions more who stayed behind working plantations as enslaved people to make sure the Confederate army had cotton in order to finance the war effort and food. To be sure, the war would not have lasted as long as it did and the successes of the Confederate army from 1861-1863 would not have been as prevalent had there not been African Americans at the very forefront of those endeavors. Far from being passive observers, African Americans were, and always have been, participants in the world surrounding them in a myriad of ways. Arnold's book is important because it takes us on this journey and helps us process the complexity and beauty of the African-American experience.

Arnold's journey of coming to grips with this history is both powerful, moving, gripping and, at times, both sad and side-splittingly funny. He teases out this complexity by taking us on that journey with him. We go with him to family reunions, to The University of Mississippi, to Nashville, to his living room, through his research and into his very own thoughts as he comes to a stark realization: "My ancestor was owned by Nathan Bedford Forrest [a man whose legacy I despise], but whom my ancestor loved." Further, he comes to understand that Forrest became a Christian: "The man who is notorious for the massacre at Fort Pillow, for serving as the Grand Wizard of the KKK and for participating in the convict-lease system (which unfairly imprisoned African Americans during Reconstruction in order to make profit off their labor) shares in a heavenly citizenship and brotherhood with me, Al Arnold. On top of this, it is possible that he loved my ancestor and my ancestor loved him." This is a very, very difficult realization to process and one that speaks to the complexities and difficulties of processing race, Southern culture and American history. It also speaks to the diversity and beauty of creation and how God has worked in our past and deals with us in the present.

How else could one explain this fact: an African-American descendant of Confederate veterans who supports the Confederate flag has asked, because of shared fellowship in Christ, a White descendent of Confederate veterans who does not support the flag to write a foreword for his book about his Confederate heritage. That fact alone displays the need for books like this and for the importance of a larger dialogue on race and history. Documenting Arnold's journey will be incredibly beneficial so that others can begin to take their own voyages. Both African Americans and Whites could stand a reevaluation of their cultures and heritages. African Americans could benefit, as Arnold does, by thinking through more deeply their potential Confederate heritage. Likewise, Whites in the South, like myself, could benefit from thinking in more nuanced ways about how their Confederate heritage has fomented racial discord and division. We could all benefit from seeing God's hand move in history in powerful ways to display to us that the world is far more complex and, simultaneously, more interwoven than we could ever possibly imagine.

Might Arnold's book take you on a journey that you never expected to go on. May it change us all to look at our shared history and to our fellow man with renewed eyes and cause us all, like the Psalmist, to say: "How good and pleasant it is when brothers dwell together in unity!"

Otis W. Pickett, Ph.D.
Professor of History, Mississippi College

About the Book

Al Arnold is a descendent of a slave, Turner Hall, Jr. "Uncle Turner," as he was known in his later years, served in the Confederate army as a body servant for two Confederate soldiers and an orderly for Robert E. Lee. As a slave, Turner Hall, Jr. was owned by another prominent Civil War general, Nathan Bedford Forrest.

Al began researching his ancestor's life in 2008. At a family reunion, he saw a newspaper caption indicating his ancestor, Turner Hall, Jr. served Robert E. Lee as an orderly in the Civil War. To Al's amazement, his research found a proud Black Confederate who held both Civil War generals in high esteem, even well after the war. At the age of ninety-five, Turner Hall, Jr. cherished a gift from Nathan Bedford Forrest as one of his most treasured possessions.

Al was further intrigued that his great-great-grandfather was a celebrated man in his community of Hugo, Oklahoma. He was commemorated as Hugo's "most distinguished citizen" by Blacks and Whites as a result of his Civil War service. Turner Hall, Jr. lived to be a hundred and four years old. He attended the last Civil War reunion in 1938 at Gettysburg, Pennsylvania.

Newsreel cameramen captured him displaying his reunion medals as an example of the typical Black Confederate.

In 1940 he was interviewed as a Black Confederate by a nationwide talk radio show in New York City. Turner Hall, Jr. left a trail for his family that Al has uncovered. Al shares his personal journey into his Confederate heritage as a modern Black man. He makes a connection through the life of his ancestor and embraces the premises that history should unite us instead of divide us. He argues that African Americans dishonor their ancestors by attempting to destroy Confederate heritage and by neglecting the historical impact that slaves had on both sides of the Civil War. These are the honest thoughts of a modern Black man who has wrestled with his Confederate heritage while being a Black Christian man in America and who is connected to two famous Civil War generals.

DEDICATION

To my grandparents, Lucian "Ras" and Arine Elliott Arnold

May you forever be remembered for the grace you shared with us: always seeking to love and forgive, teaching us the art of listening to people who were very different than we are, honoring our ancestors by working hard, honoring our word, being accepting of all kinds of people, and caring for the least among us. Above all, you were constant in demonstrating faith in Christ before us and pursuing reconciliation in all things through Him. May the Arnold and Elliott family forever seek to preserve our family history and to live according to your principles.

PREFACE

When I started researching my great-great-grandfather eight years ago, little did I know I would become a changed man. Finding information on a slave ancestor is harder than finding a needle in a haystack. However, I was given a special lens through the eyes of one incredible ancestor, Turner Hall, Jr. My discovery of his Confederate claims intensified my desire to know more about the man. As a result, I have grown from being a skeptic of Confederate heritage to a defender of that cause.

Although Black history has always been a subject of intense excitement for me, I must admit that my zeal of being connected to a Black Confederate had to grow over time. For a modern Black man, the very thought of a Black Confederate can be repulsive. Proudly, as a result of embracing this dilemma through the eyes of my great-great-grandfather, this journey has brought me to a deeper appreciation of who I am as an African American. It has heightened my love for history and the unique roles that African Americans played throughout the development of this great country. I am hopeful that African Americans will learn to embrace the vital era of the Civil War. Embracing our history, instead of rejecting it, will be the bridge that allows our society and communities to heal and grow. I'm thankful that I have had this wonderful growing experience.

ACKNOWLEDGMENTS

I want to thank my dad, Tommie Arnold, and his siblings, Uncle Eugene (Emma Jean), Willie (Pat), Earnest (Mary Nell), Herbert (Curmie), Davis, Ralph (Priscilla), aunt Pearl (Willie), Avis (Aldophus); and my deceased uncles, Emmitt and Leroy (not forgotten). Every year for the past fifteen years, they have hosted our family reunion. Family has been the main focus of our gatherings and their efforts. They have shown the next generation how to serve, love, and forgive. They did not hide the claims of their great-grandfather. Nor have they ever hidden any birth claims in the family. They celebrated his history in the Civil War and our history as his ancestors. In doing this, they have afforded the entire family and me a richer understanding of our ancestor and who he was as a person. This has brought us to a better understanding of who we have become as a family. Thanks to aunt Pearl, our Senior Family Historian. Her assistance and previous years of work on our family history made this possible.

The spark of this work was greatly enhanced and stimulated as a result of the research, support, and findings through the Oklahoma Historical Society. I cannot thank their staff enough for the wonderful assistance they have provided in this development. Thanks to my friend, Don Hubele, for your invaluable input and help with revisions. Diana Thornton of Crescent Music Services was a God send. She saved me from falling over the mountaintop of this experience.

Moreover, to my dear Confederate brothers of the SCV, "Rankin Rough & Ready's Camp #265" in Brandon, Mississippi, warm thanks for the welcome I have received from the first day I came into your midst. Your commitment to history, Confederate heritage, including the role of Blacks in the Confederacy is to be highly commended. And to my friends in the Jackson Civil War Roundtable, thank you for your support and fellowship. Your commitment to the same is highly regarded.

Finally, to my wife and kids who have stood by me in this Confederate journey. Wow! Only you really know how long, intriguing, exacerbating, and, at times, frustrating all of this has been for me. You have not only tolerated my zeal for history, the Civil War, and family, you have allowed me to be me. From my love of bluegrass music to my undying devotion to my Confederate heritage, what a ride you guys have been on. Thanks for the Civil War books, bluegrass and country music, and the listening ears over the years. But most of all, thanks for accepting all of me, including the Confederate in me.

My Formative Years

"There was an old man, his name was Uncle Ned, he died long– long– ago. He had no hair on the top of his head, the place where the wool ought to grow.

"Lay down the shovel and the hoe, pick up the fiddle and the bow, there's no more work for poor Uncle Ned, he is gone where the good darkies go, he is gone where the good darkies go. (Chorus)

"His fangers was long, like the cane in da break, he had no eyes to see. He had no teeth to eat the hoe cake, so he had to let the hoe cake be." (Chorus)

This is a slave song handed down to my family by my maternal grandmother. Growing up as a child, my family loved to sing the lyrics of "Uncle Ned."

This song was my only direct lens into the eyes of a slave. It was about a man, Uncle Ned. I pictured Uncle Ned as a strong-framed man with a worn-out body due to hard labor. He was full of wisdom and highly regarded. He was a man strong in stature. A man that was so vital to his community, a song was put to words to remember him. His meals were meager but satisfying. His eyes were dim and he had very strong hands that could grip a knot in a young boy. He was a good man.

Slaves were musically inclined and celebrations were woven into their social structure. Slaves longed to be free and heaven was certainly an option. Indeed, heaven was their freedom. I've often wondered if singing about that fiddle, at such a young age, is the reason that bluegrass is my favorite music. After I discovered the banjo hails from the continent of Africa, I realized that I had every right to bluegrass than any hillbilly in Kentucky. It was just in my bones. None of the slave narratives in school made me feel good about slavery. Uncle Ned gave me a different glimpse. It didn't take away the gore of slavery but it did give me a different perspective. It was a perspective of hope. Yet, Uncle Ned was a fictional character. Or, was he? I wasn't sure. He was a slave in a song.

Years later I would learn of another slave named Uncle Turner. The only difference was that this uncle was not a fictional character in a song. He was my great-great-grandfather. This discovery would begin my journey into my Confederate heritage.

It was at a family reunion in 2008 when my Aunt Pearl revealed our family heritage book. In that book was a photo that I had seen many times. But there was something else that struck me as remarkably odd. There was a caption from a newspaper article, "Turner Hall, A Real Pioneer" that read, "During the Civil War, Uncle Turner was an orderly for Robert E. Lee."

As a young African-American boy growing up in northeast Mississippi, history was always a favorite subject during my formative years. Having a photographic memory, I devoured essay questions on American and Mississippi history exams. History surrounding wars was especially interesting to me. I marveled at historical figures and embraced stories of personal triumph and heroism. The one figure that I regretted, as a very young historian, was Benedict Arnold. The fact that he was a known traitor during the American Revolution and carried my last name gave me chills. I was fearful that one day I would come to learn that he was my ancestor.

Ancestry has always been intriguing to me. What human being doesn't want to know where he comes from? I believe I am not alone in this quest. If the truth were told, many African Americans want to know more about their ancestors. However, records are so vague in our history. Records only go so far due to historical issues of how slaves were considered property and not people. It's only so far that we can go back and then we hit that inevitable wall of slavery that we all know is there. So, many just never muster up the energy to start. As much as I would love to go further than I have, I find a bit of relief that I will never be able to trace a connection of my name to the most familiar traitor in American history: Benedict Arnold. So, in a sense, I am protected. Shielded from the shame. Indeed, the shame of it all is enough to stop the most resourceful person in their pursuit of their own personal ancestry.

Yet, as a young boy, nothing intrigued me more than personal family history. I was raised during a time when bravery was inspirational and heroism was awarded at great sacrifice. My mother's family consisted of a matriarch and eight daughters. My father's family consisted of a patriarch, matriarch, ten boys, and two girls. There are countless cousins and extended family members that came from these family trees. During those years, photos were a tangible way for most families to keep record. There was no better way in my family to review our history than to ask my grandmother to show the family portraits. She kept them in a cedar chest in her home. It would be years later that we would learn the value of cedar wood. The house burned, destroying all of her possessions except those priceless photos preserved by the cedar. It was in those photos that I first saw a picture of my great-great-grandfather, Turner Hall, Jr., the inspiration of this book. I didn't know his name at the time and not much was said about him. I remember him being a grand figure of a man. He was tall, handsome, and had a pleasant disposition, much unlike the many faces of the old photos of his day. I remember him standing proudly with an alarmingly huge hat and a dazzling blue jacket with large buttons on each side. He stood with a large frame in front of what appeared to be a row of very small white homes. My grandmother would say, "That's my Papa." This photo, I later learned was her mother's father and my great-great-grandfather, Turner Hall, Jr.

Time and time again we would sit on the floor and she would pull out photos and allow us to look and ask questions.

We usually didn't touch the photos. These photos demanded respect and the best behavior. At the time, we didn't know where she kept the photos. She would always make us stay in the front room as she retrieved the photos from the cedar chest. Another great family photo of superb importance and personality to the family was of my grandfather's father, Lucian "Paw Dick" Arnold. This photo, like that of Turner Hall, Jr., is etched in the memory of all the Arnold clan. In the photo, "Paw Dick" is sitting in a chair with his wooden peg leg and a huge cigar in his mouth—exuding nothing but pride, sincerity, and character. An annual review and conversation of these two photos and many more were like a ritual for elders in the family and a right of passage for all youngsters. The fruits and labor of these two men would define who we were and who we would aspire to be as individuals of this family. Their pictures portrayed self-esteem, hard work, honesty, faithfulness, forwardness, faith, perseverance, hope, and integrity. Their kids would be beacon lights in the eyes and hearts of the next two generations of Arnolds. A thread of family loyalty and history were established around these photos and family gatherings that continue to this day. The annual family reunion at the homefront in Monroe County, Mississippi, is much like a yearly community celebration.

When I was a young man, having been firmly established by strong family connections through Christian values, personal responsibility and strong work ethics from both sides of the family, it was time to depart home and pursue a college education. My parents were among the working poor; cut off from opportunities largely due to dropping out of high school. This was the case with many Blacks and Whites in rural Mississippi. Hard work was a viable option in their day and that is what they pursued. They worked by the sweat of their brow. My mom worked in a wood factory making doors and my father worked in a meat processing company. Mother, many years later, obtained a GED and went on to graduate from college. My father, without an education, worked his way up to head plant manager and supervised the entire night shift operation at a huge processing plant. He told me once that he never worked a job that he didn't quickly find himself as supervisor. With only a few exceptions, I represented the first generation of family members to leave home to pursue a college degree. I soon realized how privileged I was to have such an opportunity.

At this time in my life, I begin to think of the historical implications of the plight of my family and those who had prevailed many hardships. Furthermore, what was I to make of my forefathers? They knew nothing but hard work. Who were these men and how did they leave such strong family ties? It was also during these years that I first became familiar with the historical aspects of slavery, the Confederacy, and the implication of these issues upon the African American, the State of Mississippi, the South, and this country. Having chosen a historical Black college and university in Jackson, Mississippi, Jackson State University, I embarked upon areas of learning that offered historical nuances unique to the African-American experience. This was a solid start that would prepare me for a life in the South. My high school guidance counselor had warned me that if I attended a Black college, I would learn to hate White people. Well, one thing that I did not learn at JSU was to hate White people. However, what I did learn was to think critically of other Black folk and to come to the realization that some Black folks are just as crazy as some White folks.

Next was a largely all-White experience at the School of Physical Therapy at the University of Mississippi, just across town from Jackson State. I left JSU and graduated as the only African-American male in a class of forty-two graduates in the School of Physical Therapy in 1991. Although there were a few JSU professors and many of my peers who deemed Ole Miss off limits during that time, most professors encouraged students to go to Ole Miss, if accepted, to show that we were capable of competing. I remember the pressure of being the only Black male in my physical therapy class. There were two Black females in my class. It was really tough at one point. I was doing so well in school and actually thought everybody in the school had to think I was cheating. My White peers thought I was a Black genius and had me over for dinner many nights. That served a poor boy like me well during those days. What they didn't know is that I had studied every aspect of anatomy the previous summer months and had memorized every bone, muscle, and nerve in the body; I could name them and recall everything about them with my eyes closed before the first class.

I went on to graduate from Ole Miss with honors. I was voted the most outstanding student by the faculty and received the "Minority Scholarship of Academic Excellence" for the highest academic GPA of all minority students in America from the American Physical Therapy Association (I was the first African American to receive the award in 1990). I can only recall one negative racial experience during my enrollment at the University of Mississippi. It was not among my classmates and surprisingly, at the time, didn't come from my faculty. I had the best support from the faculty while at Ole Miss and later realized that some of the stereotypes about going to any of the branches of the University medical schools wasn't an issue of getting in. The real issue was could you successfully get out? When I got into the Physical Therapy program, I learned that the administrators at the school were more concerned about graduating students successfully rather than having an easy open-door policy of admission. Because of this, admission standards were very high and highly competitive.

After college, I moved to New Orleans for six months but soon returned to Mississippi. Kissing the ground, I vowed never to leave her again. From that day to now, I always refer to my beloved state as, "The Great State of Mississippi!"

The War that Made a New People

I can't count the times I've used the expression, "You can't choose your family, you're born into it." My mom once told me that only God gets you out of a thing, over a thing, and through a thing without changing a thing. In some regard, the War Between the States, from the perspective of most African Americans my age, is perfectly summed up in this statement. These are our sentiments of the hundred years after the war. Our people got out of slavery and made it over the next hundred years and suffered throughout the process—but the issue had not changed. The slave received his freedoms with the 13th, 14th, and 15th amendments but did not fully see the fruition of those amendments for another hundred years after the Civil War.

Let's put that in perspective for an African American such as myself. In my research, I discovered that my great-great-grandfather returned to Okolona, Mississippi after the war. The Civil War ended in 1865. I was born in Okolona, Mississippi in 1968. That's a hundred and three years later. The year I was born was one of the most turbulent times during the civil rights movement for African Americans. It was the year Dr. Martin Luther King, Jr. was killed. By the time I became a grown man, I had to develop a perspective and appreciation for those who had struggled during the civil rights movement. I certainly hadn't developed critical thoughts of the Civil War preceding this era, though the historical connections were later evident to me. My questions of the hundred-year gap were largely relegated to mystery. I wanted badly to fill this void. It was like the gap between the Old Testament and the New Testament. There is a total disconnect to the Civil War for African Americans in my generation. We learned little, if anything, of the Negro role in the war. For my generation, slavery represented the Old Testament. The hundred years after the war represents the gap in which God did not speak (between the Old and New Testament). The civil rights movement was our New Testament. It was our beginning. Yet, the actual historical beginning had come a hundred years previously. Out of darkness and confusion God waited four hundred years to set in motion events that would be the making of a people. It was the Civil War. I have come to appreciate that this making of a people was not only for former slaves but for former slave owners as well. Redemption and freedom would come to both people and forge a nation of greatness.

Therefore, I believe this hundred-year gap is a primary cause of disconnect between today's contemporary Negro and the Civil War. I would suspect for Whites my age, the same could be said. The only difference is many Whites have recorded historical connections. On the other hand, African Americans my age know nothing about the Civil War because of the hundred-year gap. Whites my age will quickly tell you they had nothing to do with slavery. This is the tension that has existed over the past fifty years for adults my age. In essence, African Americans my age don't want to know about slavery and our White peers don't want to be blamed for slavery. That leaves only two factions to dialogue over the most important war of our country. Those who are trying to hold on to their rightful Confederate heritage and those that were abused during the civil rights era of our country seeking their rightful civil rights as a people.

Who doesn't want God on their side? Not only did the North and South believe that God was on their side, the slaves fervently believed that God was on their side. Southerners saw their plight just as the early founding fathers of our country saw themselves fighting to be liberated from British rule. It was not a rebellion but a revolution. Thus, just as God had caused a rag-tag militia group of civilians to prevail against the British army, so too would He cause the South to prevail against the tyrannical rule of the Northern government? Abolitionist and radical Northern Republicans saw the South as an immoral aristocracy and claimed God to be defenders of their cause. Abolitionist John Brown said:

> "I am now quite certain that the crimes of this guilty land will never be purged away; but with Blood. I had as I now think vainly flattered myself that

without very much bloodshed, it might be done."
(John Brown, Charleston, VA Dec. 2nd, 1859)

The Civil War, in my opinion, is the war of all wars for our country. It is this war that is mostly responsible for who we are as a nation. Because of this war, we became a successful nation militarily, socially, and spiritually. Of course, the social advancement was delayed for millions. Military tactics from the Civil War were incorporated in World War I and World War II. Had it not been for the Civil War, Hitler may have very well prevailed. Many of our land grant colleges, including the historical Black Alcorn State University in Lorman, Mississippi, are a result of the legislation immediately following the Civil War. The 13th, 14th, and 15th amendments giving former slaves their freedom, equal rights, and protection of the laws and a right to vote respectively came as a direct result of the Civil War. As an African American, I am compelled to study this war like none other. Perhaps no other human race has been discredited in the annals of wartime history than the Negro. Although, unquestionably, there is no American war that he cannot be found to have participated in and yet his efforts are usually minimized in significance. From the Revolutionary War to the Civil War, there he was, fighting, serving, and dying for a struggle. The struggle for the Negro, until this point in modern history, usually involved loyalty, courage, servanthood, and manhood. As much as I want to believe my ancestor raised an army of slaves, escaped north, and joined the Northern army, that didn't happen. Perhaps these are the hopes of many contemporary African Americans. The hope of many would be to dream of heroism that aligns with their current ideology. However, the Negro slave was much more complex than that. Although, some did have the opportunity to escape on the back of the Union army and through other routes, many never came into close proximity of a Union military. For those who were fortunate enough to trail behind a Union regiment, many were abandoned, suffered for lack of food and shelter, and were often sold back into slavery or killed.

Many slaves would fight with their boyhood masters. At the start of the war, in particularly, there was no promise of freedom attached to the victor of the war. No promises had been granted to the Negro that would have led him to believe if he fought on either side of the conflict that he would be better off. Overwhelmingly, neither the South nor the North employed soldiers in the beginning of the war. By the end of the war, both sides either had used Negro soldiers or had passed legislation to incorporate Negro soldiers. However, that doesn't mean the Negro was doing nothing, as often betrayed by modern African-American thought. He was not standing by watching White folks fight. They were intimately involved in various ways. They served as scouts, spies, cooks, blacksmiths, trench diggers, and a host of other support roles. Some were calvary men, regular soldiers, and snipers. The Negro was the master forager on either side of the war. In fact, the entire Confederate army was supported by an infrastructure of Black men who served throughout the war. Contrary to what many African Americans believe, Abraham Lincoln did as much as he could to stabilize slavery in the southern states as any Southerner. Moreover, slaves were not welcomed in the North. White Northerners during the war were often more racist than Southerners toward Blacks. Here is a capture of what happened to Blacks in New York City after the fall of Vicksburg and Port Hudson:

> "The mob was composed of the lowest and most degraded of the foreign population (mainly Irish), raked from the filthy cellars and dens of the city, steeped in crimes of the deepest dye, and ready for any act, no matter how dark and damnable; together with the worst type of our native criminals, whose long service in prisons of the country, and whose training in the Democratic party, had so demoralized their natures, that they were ever on the hunt for some deed of robbery or murder. Never, in the history of mob-violence, was crime carried to such an extent. Murder, arson, robbery, and cruelty reigned triumphant throughout the city, day and night, for more than a week. Hundreds of the Blacks, driven from their homes, and hunted and chased through the streets, presented themselves at the doors of jails, prisons, and police stations, and begged admission. Thus did they prowl about the city, committing crime after crime; indeed, in point

of cruelty, the Rebellion was transferred from the South to the North." (Wells Brown, *The Negro in The American Rebellion*, Chapter XXVI–1867)

Many of the Union generals had no tolerance for Negros. General Tecumseh Sherman in particular had a strong disdain for the Negro. Any serious student of history knows that Lincoln used the issue of slavery as a prop to lure the Southern states back into the Union. His primary goal was to preserve the Union, not to free the slaves. Had he had his way, the South could have kept their slaves. Lincoln was not a member of the Radical Republicans that promoted the Civil War as an end to slavery. Yet, we don't see this version of Lincoln portrayed in the 2012 movie, Lincoln. We see him as the great deliverer of the slave. African Americans did not hesitate to support this movie nor did they protest Lincoln's pro-Southern views. Should we remove Abraham Lincoln's portrait from the five-dollar bill? If we follow the logic of some modern African Americans to remove every vestige and symbol of those who supported slavery we would have to destroy the North much as the north destroyed the South during the Civil War. Is that a logical thing to do? Is that an absurd thought? Of course it is illogical to think this way.

A very high percentage of Mississippi Confederate regiments had Negro servants at the time of their departure. My great-great-grandfather is noted to have "flunked" for two

Confederate soldiers. As a result, many young Negros departed with the sons of their master or their master themselves. These same servants would stay by their masters' sides throughout the war. Many would go to great extremes to find the dead bodies of their comrades to ensure that the body was returned home for proper burial.

Has Birthday - Turner Hall

"Uncle Turner Hall has taken the spotlight for being Hugo's most distinguished resident.

The one hundred year old colored man was born October 10th, 1840, a slave on a Mississippi Plantation and was therefore a century old last Friday.

Has Birthday

Turner Hall

Uncle Turner Hall has taken the spotlight for being Hugo's most distinguished resident.
The one hundred year old colored man was born October 10th. 1840, a slave on a Mississippi plantation and was therefore a century old last Friday.
In June 1938, he was honored by the United States government and given a free trip to the last Civil war veterans reunion at Gettysburg. Virginia and was again honored by appearing on the "We, the People" nation-wide radio hock up in New York sponsored by the Sanka Coffee company, in May this year.
Uncle Turner was brought to Hugo from Mississippi many years ago and has resided here ever since.
Uncle Turner is a civil war veteran, having served in the southern army and was orderly for General Robert E. Lee commander of the southern armies and was present when Gen. Lee surrendered to General Grant.
His memory is excellent and he enjoys relating his experiences in connection with his services for the famous southern general.
His claims to this distinction have been verified from records in the war department.

In June 1938 he was honored by the United States government and given a free trip to the last Civil war veterans reunion at Gettysburg, Virginia and was again honored by appearing on the "We, the People" nation-wide radio hock up in New York sponsored by the Sanka Coffee company, in May this year.

Uncle Turner was brought to Hugo from Mississippi many years ago and has resided here ever since. Uncle Turner is a Civil War veteran, having served in the southern army and was orderly for General Robert E. Lee commander of the southern armies and was present when Gen. Lee surrendered to General Grant.

His memory is excellent and he enjoys relating his experiences in connection with his services for the famous southern general.

His claims to this distinction have been verified from records in the war department." (*Hugo Daily News* October 13, 1940. Oklahoma Historical Society)

MY BELOVED MISSISSIPPI & THE CONFEDERATE FLAG

Charles Rangel, Democrat Congressman in New York, quickly became a notable Black politician that I didn't like for his comments, particularly his, "who in the hell wants to live in Mississippi" comment in 2006. At the time of his comment, I was thirty-seven years old. I fired back at the TV and yelled, "Who in the hell wants to live in New York, Charlie?" He later apologized and I had to come to grips with what I thought he meant in his famous blasphemy against the hospitality state. I took him not to mean anything derogative toward the people of Mississippi. In fact, he released a statement verifying his intent was not to offend anyone. "I just love New York so much that I can't understand why everyone wouldn't want to live here." My sentiments exactly! Regarding the great state of Mississippi, we have it all. Good living, fishing, hunting, great food, the best music, and hospitality. I like to say that most of everything good in every other state got its start in Mississippi:. "Keep your city life, Charlie, I'll take the country any day!"

Needless to say, we do have our history. Yet, because of that history, we are far ahead in some regards. One of the hot political issues of the state that would often come up was the issue of the state flag. Once again, I would remember a warning that my high school guidance counselor gave me when I told her I would attend Jackson State University. "You will learn to hate White folks if you go to that college." I never understood her at the time. One reason is because of the close relationships that I had with my fellow White friends in high school. For the most part, we lived on different sides of town. Both sides of town were largely poor, hard-working folks. We grew up together at school, played sports together, and our parents largely worked in the same factories. My high school years were as diverse as they could have been, though looking back we had separate Black and White proms, Black and White football queens, Black and White class favorites, and the likes. The problem was, we didn't know it was a problem, so it never was. We were just as happy for the White queen as we were for the Black one. After the big game, we all would get together in our separate groups and go visit the other groups to see what was going on over there. We had our fun on both sides of town. I guess the administrators somehow thought they were protecting us, or perhaps themselves. On Saturday nights, there was a place where the Whites hung out and there was a place where the Blacks hung out. Neither location was considered off grounds for either group. If we wanted to go see our White friends we knew exactly where to go, and the same was true of them.

So, when it came to the state flag of Mississippi, I never understood why I couldn't get dialed up about it. One of the things I learned was the moment you forget history, you are doomed to repeat it. For this reason, I thought, for better or worse, it was best to leave the state flag alone. Now, I must admit, I was probably in the minority on this view and didn't march to keep it flying high but my reasons were solid enough not to change my position. Let the rebels have their flag. It means something to them. At the time my position was this, "Find something that means something for you and stand up for it just as the rebel." Take it down and it means nothing! How can it mean nothing when it is a part of history? My thought was clear. Every symbol means something. Find out what it means to you and deal with it. Don't try to hinder what it may mean to someone else. For me, history was important. Even the most shameful moments in history take on different meanings for different folks. The good or bad of it all can point us to a better future. But if I forget why I dislike something because I no longer see it or if I forget why I love something because I no longer see it, what good is this?

On many national issues we may find ourselves separated but one thing you will soon realize in Mississippi is that Black folks and White folks have been at this race thing for a long time. We know how to talk to each other, work with each other, and go to school with each other. That doesn't mean that we don't have areas of our state that are challenged in many of these same regards. Contrary to the many outside stereotypes of the state, you will find more friendships merged across racial lines in this state than you will enemies.

Culture is Not Racism: Martin's Dream

Brotherly Love

"The sons of former slaves and the sons of former slave owners will be able to sit down together at the table of brotherhood." (MLK, Jr., '63)

Cultural Diversity

"Little black boys and black girls will be able to join hands with little white boys and white girls as sisters and brothers." (MLK, Jr., '63)

The Good White Folk

"For many of our white brothers, as evidenced by their presence here today, have come to realize that their destiny is tied up with our destiny." (MLK, Jr., '63)

We Cannot Walk Alone

And as we walk, we must make the pledge that we shall always march ahead. We cannot turn back." (MLK, Jr., '63)

Cultural differences are not always indicative of racism. Cultural differences are an expression of who a people are and have become because of experiences and geographical locations endowed upon them by Almighty God. The Confederate

Southern heritage is as legitimate and tangible as the Negro's demands for certain foods rooted in his heritage. Let me be more specific. I don't know a people in the annals of time that love to eat hog chitterlings more so than the Black man. When we gather to fill ourselves with the delicacy of such delight, we are experiencing and embracing deep cultural roots that are rooted in our history. I simply will not be denied my annual right to indulge myself with as much of this God-given grace than I can hold. On the other hand, my delight could very well serve as disgust to some. Let them frown and sneer at me as if I am inhuman to consume such goods and I will simply have another bowl. You mess with a Black man's chitterlings and you will have hell to pay! Now, we very well know that everything about this great prize is not good or healthy or even sane to prepare. However, certain times of the year, families will make their journeys to fulfill the ultimate quest of getting the best hog guts their money can buy. Certainly, all do not indulge. But it is unique to the Black man's story as much as the rebel flag and all of its history is to the Confederate heritage. I don't compare apple and oranges. I compare heritage and culture. They are uniquely different for groups of people and they are expressed in various ways. A Flag has many meanings for different folks. That will never change. My ancestor was a servant under the Confederate flag. I can find no record of anything but admiration of that fact on his behalf. I suspect he would not have been the only one who would have had the experience of being a part of a war that would shake the history of our modern country.

No one can deny the existence of racism in America. Any institution that is governed to suppress and oppress a people cannot be labeled anything but what it is. They also understand that slavery was in existence throughout the world and was a practice in many societies. The United States of America was no exception. The overwhelming majority of my Confederate brothers and sisters agree that slavery was outright wrong. The Confederate flag does not indicate a racist any more than the cross indicates a Christian.

To suggest that having a White prom and a Black prom at one high school is racist doesn't fully comprehend the important role of culture and the importance of race. That doesn't mean that we don't acknowledge that these practices may have derived from impure motives. Perhaps not so much today as it was in my day, Black folks and White folks listened to very different music, danced in very different ways, and had very different social norms. Again, this is not to deny that separation of races for such events, in former times, didn't have roots in racial identity and they may have evolved from racism. But to suggest that because these events were separate was inherently racist is wrong. As much as we loved our White classmates and were loved by them, we also loved our culture so much that we enjoyed our differences without allowing them to destroy our love for each other. Not to mention that at no time was anyone turned away from a White prom or a Black prom because they happened to show up at the wrong prom. We were genuinely happy to stop by each other's prom to share in the different cultural experience. This was well before we knew anything about cultural diversity. By some God-given desire, we were experiencing it. God made diversity and we have certainly had to grow to understand this over time. Perhaps it has been harder for one group to come to grips with this than another. However, now that we understand and value diversity and different cultural experiences, we now must embrace the old Southern Confederate culture as one that is as authentic and God given as any other. This is what has shaped a large segment of the Southern hospitality that is very common in this part of God's country among Blacks and Whites. The Blacks that are descendants of the slaves who stayed in the South are as much part of this Confederate hospitality as anyone. What do we think happened to all of the culture the slaves absorbed in the South? Do we really think that all of the "soul food" in the South developed post-civil rights movement? What about the notion that Sunday dinner at grandmother's house is a cultural norm of Black folks that started in the '70s? I contend that everything good about the South (Black and White) came from the old South just as much as anywhere else. This hospitality went north during the great migration of Negroes. Hard work, honesty, humility, strength, and integrity went north as well. At the same time, a lot of it stayed south, close to the homeland.

Martin Luther King, Jr. had a dream before I was born that I would one day sit down with a Confederate brother and break bread at his table. I should not expect him to be any less of a Confederate than he is to expect me to be less Black. I have never sat on a red hill in Georgia but the red clay of Mississippi will do just fine. I think it is blissful that King would be able to see that the reunion of the slave master and the slave would occur in the immediate territory of their common ground. No new land would be established. Instead, new hearts would emerge in the same old land.

One of my first experiences of approaching my Confederacy came in the home of a patient that I cared for in rural Mississippi. There I was marveling at the distinct Southern culture that I found myself in. I knew right away that I was in deep cotton. Her husband was a true Confederate. The rebel flag flew high and the bumper sticker read, "Nathan Bedford Forrest." In my duties as a home health therapist, I have provided care for all kinds of people of different walks of life for the past six years. I know where the Confederates live and I know where the Black Nationalist lives. This guy wasn't a lukewarm Confederate. He was true in his convictions and wasn't the kindest gentleman, but a gentleman indeed. He was a hard-shell Confederate. It must have been two weeks before I could get him to have a conversation. Part of the problem was it was election time and Barack Obama was running for his second term. I was a Black man in a Southerner's home with Fox News blasting anti-Obama lyrics. I was staring in the face of one of the meanest damn rebels I had ever met. I knew this one would be hard, so I decided to wait him out. He said nothing and neither did I. Meanwhile, that beautiful Southern lady and I carried on as if we had known each other for years. Being her therapist was a joy, but I must say, I took note not to make her holler too much when stretching that shoulder. The old man was never really out of reach. The final day came and I decided to go all in. I would break the silence in a way that I knew would either get me a solid cursing or would open up a deep dialogue. Up until this point, I had not disclosed my Confederate ties. I jumped right in when the door opened. It had become apparent to me that he was not going to turn Fox News off. I even think he turned it up when I walked through the door. I asked the question, "Who are they going to get to beat Obama this time? There is no way you good Southern Baptists are going to vote for a Mormon for president?" Well, that did it. He jumped off of that couch and that was the first time I had ever heard the term, "damn rag head!" He was referring to Obama, of course, and the silence was over. We talked politics, Civil War, and Nathan Bedford Forrest. At the time, I did not know that Forrest owned my ancestor. He disclosed to me his bitterness over land that his family had lost after the war. I could really feel his disgust in that regard. It was a victory for him and me. We had connected. Using such a hot-button dagger as the Obama dagger in the home of a rebel was risky. However, I enjoyed it so much because it was the one weapon I held that I could use to break the hardest of the hard shells. It wasn't agreement that I sought. It was dialogue. I wanted to know more about the man. I am in the people business and there was no way I was going to leave that house without finding out more about who this man was and why. That to me completed the home health visit. It makes it whole. I'm glad I took that risk. It was several years later that I came to know that Nathan Bedford Forrest owned my great-great-grandfather. I returned to the home of this gentleman. But this dear brother had passed. I often wonder, had he known what I now know, what impact would that have had on our relationship, even as brief as it was?

There is much hope in Dr. King's dream. Black girls and boys would hold hands with White girls and boys. Is this not the hope of those that cry out for a post-racial America? However, there is an interpretation of Dr. King's dream here that I think is often overlooked. When I survey his dream, I see nothing that says the Black boy and girl would no longer be Black. I also see no indication that the White boy or girl wouldn't still be White. This is diversity at best. When people can be the people that

God ordained them to be in their culture, they are at their best. Wrapped in the Confederate flag is a unique culture and heritage. I don't think I have any right to frown upon that heritage or culture any more than Confederates have a right to frown upon mine. I don't have to understand a person's culture or even agree with it in order to love them. Thus, because I am reconciled in Christ, I can allow a Confederate to be a Confederate without attacking him or her for their flag or their history. I can accept him as a Christian as much as any Christian in this land. After all, I am a part of that history. If the Jew could accept the Samaritan as a brother, who am I to not accept my Confederate brother? Moreover, my ancestor served under this banner with the pride of one doing his duty. I honestly believe he faithfully discharged those duties without prejudice and willingly. With honor, he and many other slaves stayed loyal to the Confederate nation.

My ancestor ties me directly to Confederate history in an odd and twisted way. That doesn't mean I condone slavery or wish that the Confederates had won the war to preserve slavery or establish a new nation. It just means that I am as complex as any man and the flag is one complex issue. To deny that it has been used as a symbol of hate is an outright lie. All of my Confederate friends agree to this fact and grieve this more than anyone. There is no pride in witnessing a symbol of pride and honor being used in a way that does not represent its meaning. Historically, some have taken the symbol of Christianity, the cross, and used it for warfare, cultism, slavery, and many other perversions contrary to its true meaning. Should we take down the cross because of the acts of the crusaders? Or should we rather study and learn from the crusades? I can find nowhere in the Bible that indicates that God hates history. In fact, I find just the opposite. It is HIS STORY. I believe a big part of HIS STORY is demonstrated in how well we seek the role of being our brother's keeper, which I will discuss in the last chapter. He often required monuments to remind Israel of their sin. God hates sin, not symbols. The symbol of sin is all around us but no one in our communities cry out against that as fiercely as they do against the Confederate flag. It has become an acceptable norm in African-American communities for young male adults to kill others as well as to pray upon the weak and vulnerable. At the time of this writing (June 28, 2015) there has been over a thousand shootings in Chicago alone and we are only six months into the year. At this rate it is possible to have over two thousand shooting victims in this one city for the year of 2015.

Revisionist history is taking your time horizon and historical perspective and applying it to the lens of time and history of a different era. By removing the original historical context from an object, position, or time and applying a new historical context that is specific to your time period is an incorrect way of interpreting history. Christians who are faithful to the Word of God understand this as they deal with scriptures.

A proper method of understanding the scripture is to have a full grasp of the context and historical cultural narrative in which it is given. This is helpful to ensure that we receive God's Word and not our own as we apply it to our lives. To handle scripture any other way is a violation of the first principle of faithfully sharing the Word of God. Sadly, many Christians totally fail to apply this basic principle to American History and the Civil War. It is well known that men who used the Confederate battle flag symbol to portray supremacist views and bigotry as well as to suppress Black voters brought the flag of the Confederacy back into display in the era of the civil rights. The battle flag of the Confederate army had not flown since the end of the Civil War in 1865. Yet, bigotry resurrected the Confederate flag and forever stained a symbol that had been held in a time of war as a symbol of pride and honor for Blacks and Whites that served under it.

Just like the people in Enterprise, Alabama, erecting a monument to remind them of the one thing that brought destruction to their society, the Confederate flag helps to remind me of the painful history of African Americans as well as the unity that is offered by people who are willing to look at history as a tool for learning instead of an object of bitterness. It also reminds me of the high cost and sacrifice that Confederates, Whites and Blacks, endured for the building of this country. I have discovered that my Confederate brothers are not hell bent on putting Black folk back into slavery. In fact, it's just the opposite. They will look at you and tell you flat out that slavery was wrong. Yet, their ancestors, just like mine, fought in a war that had astronomical implications for our country. The fact that many were killed in this war means that they gave the ultimate sacrifice that people can give of themselves for their country, right or wrong.

Now, we can certainly discuss and should discuss the facts of the Civil War. Did the Confederates lose the war, secede from the Union, fight for slavery versus state rights? And did slaves fight voluntarily or under compulsion for the South? Did Southerners or Northerners treat slaves better? I simply contend that there are too few African Americans who even consider these thoughts when they see a Confederate flag. Because history has been so cruel to our plight, we find ourselves without any useful historical regard to the Confederate flag. African Americans overwhelmingly have contempt of the flag because of the likes of Dylann Roof, the KKK, and the civil rights era. Hate groups taking the flag out of a larger historical context have hijacked the Confederate flag.

Hijacking of symbols or movements is not uncommon in our society. A more prevalent example is the perceived hijacking of the civil rights movement by the gay rights movement. Overwhelmingly, African Americans will conclude that being Black and being homosexual are two separate issues. A common thought among many conservative and liberal Blacks is that being Black is an issue of birth but homosexual is an issue of choice. That is the mainstream thought of African Americans, though this thought may be shifting further to the left. It doesn't take long to show that Blacks feel strongly that the civil rights movement and the gay rights movement have nothing in common. This may not be the politically correct view among Black politicians, but it is the larger private view among Blacks throughout the country.

If you associate a symbol or a movement with a new concept long enough and do it on a consistent basis, it will typically become the norm. The gay rights movement initially received strong pushback from the African-American community when the gay rights movement tagged on to the civil rights movement. African Americans became silent on the issue with the election of our first African-American president. After his first successful campaign, gays became a political aid not only to the president, but also to African Americans. Because of the gay rights movement's support of the president, Blacks sympathized more with their cause and relinquished their cry of foul play. Anyone that could help us help the president stay in office had a pass to lay claim to the civil rights movement. This was an awkward feeling in the Deep South for African Americans. The Black Bible belt is extremely strong in the South. There are four churches in almost every neighborhood.

African Americans have historically been very conservative when it comes to issues of homosexuality. Yet, we never dreamed of the reality of having an African-American president. If it takes being silent about an issue such as gay rights, then that is just what we were going to have to do.

Nothing, and I do mean nothing, can our beloved president be wrong about. Maybe a little off on this gay rights thing but never wrong. So, Black people extended him grace in this area. We reasoned that White men had been in that office all this time and they haven't been right about everything. This doesn't really hurt us. We don't agree with him but we won't be loud about it.

I remember the first time I heard President Obama speak. I had heard so much about this promising African-American guy named Obama. I had just received a phone call from a family member joking that whoever this guy Obama was he'd have to change his name because America would never elect a person with the last name Obama. Well, I had to see for myself. I finally caught the guy during a pre-election speech. I will never forget my response. I jumped off the couch and started running and yelling so loud that my family thought we had a burglar. I screamed in laughter and joy and said to my wife, "We haven't had a Negro speak like that since Martin Luther King, Jr. We have our first Black president!" He had two beautiful young daughters at the time and my boys were excited that one day they would get to meet them. I remember my youngest was fascinated. He asked if he could one day date the man's daughter.

I said, "Boy, what would you say to the president of the United States about dating his daughter?" His reply is in the annals of our family. He said. "I will tell him: Mr. Obama, I have a dream, too!" I said, "Boy, his name is Obama, not Martin Luther King, Jr."

We all laughed and told him that his reply would have been great.

Now, speaking of the president. I don't know one of my dear Confederate brothers who agree with anything that he has done. That's their right and their perspective. I can still love them, and laugh at them and with them. We usually come to the conclusion that we are really not too far off from each other on most issues. They mention ObamaCare; I tell them to give me their Medicare card. They mention penalties, and I remind them that this was a Republican idea from the start (to tax people who weren't contributing to their cost). Ultimately, we come to one conclusion. Somehow, the politicians are getting richer but we are getting poorer. Once that point is reached, we are looking each other in the eye as men in the same boat.

But what of the Confederate flag? Are we to remove it and take it down from every vestige of America's society? Only the great State of Mississippi remains. Should it be in a museum?

Any serious student of history will find no better plight for the African American under the American flag as compared to the Confederate flag. We forget that it was the American flag that allowed slavery to thrive. For four centuries, slavery existed in America under the American flag, not the Confederate flag. We must pause to remember that at the time of the Underground Railroad, freedom was in Canada, not America. African Americans need to pause and think about that. The train stopped in Canada, not New York. And you will never see a KKK march without the prominent display of the American flag.

Make a Monument

"The monument did not showcase the boll weevil as the reason why the people of Enterprise couldn't succeed. It wasn't erected because they were displaying their excuse for failure for the world to see. It was simply saying, 'Here is what once was our problem. Here is the pest that pushed us to think different, to live different and as a result, to be successful.' (Enterprise Alabama, Coffee County erection of a monument to their problem, the Boll Weevil)

In order to inherit the promise land, the children of Israel had to cross over the Jordan. There was no underground tunnel to cross the Jordan. The Jordan River was, indeed, a problem. It was no little task ahead of them. We often forget that woman, children, elderly, and perhaps those who were handicapped had to cross. Four hundred years of oppression and it was time to cross this threshold of faith. What did God tell them to do? When you cross this river, don't ever remember it? Don't study it? Don't teach your children or mention this to them? Quite the contrary!

Joshua 4:2

"take twelve men out of the people, out of every tribe a man,"

Joshua 4:3

"And command ye them, saying, Take you hence out of the midst of Jordan, out of the place where the priests' feet stood firm, twelve stones, and ye shall carry them over with you, and leave them in the lodging place, where ye shall lodge this night."

- Make your monument out of your problems.
- Take the parts of the monument home with you.
- Place it near where you sleep.

Joshua 4:4

"Then Joshua called the twelve men, whom he had prepared of the children of Israel, out of every tribe a man,"

Joshua 4:5

"And Joshua said unto them, Pass over before the ark of the LORD your God into the midst of Jordan, and take ye up every man of you a stone upon his shoulder, according unto the number of the tribes of the children of Israel."

Your children are going to ask you later about your monument.

Joshua 4:6

"That this may be a sign among you, that when your children ask their fathers in time to come, saying, What mean ye by these stones?

Joshua 4:7

"Then ye shall answer them, That the waters of Jordan were cut off before the ark of the covenant of the LORD; when it passed over Jordan, the waters of Jordan were cut off: and these stones shall be for a memorial unto the children of Israel forever.
"These stones declared, 'There once was an obstacle in front of us that we couldn't get over. But God made a way. We never want to forget.'"

A biblical example of this is the rainbow. God left us a sign that he would never destroy the earth with water again. Out of the ugly destruction of His earth, He left a beautiful reminder to symbolize His promise. In some regard, I see the Confederate flag as that kind of symbol for me. I want to see it, if not daily, frequently, to remind me what God has done and that those days will never be seen again. On the other hand, the flag is a lasting tribute to my ancestor and his role in the war. Either way, to God be the glory.

African Americans need to start owning their history. We should make monuments instead of tearing them down. Instead of politicians, movie stars, and professional athletes tearing down history, they should be using their influence to build it up. History is important. It doesn't matter how you feel about it. History is objective, not subjective. The fact that Christ died on a cross over 2,000 years ago is an objective historical fact. It doesn't matter what you feel about it. Your feelings don't change that objective historical event. I don't ever want to forget my ancestors, my heritage, culture—our past. I don't ever want to forget the Civil War and those who fought in it. Before the 2014 movie *The Help*" many young African Americans never knew the role of African-American women who were caring for White children in the '50s to '60s. African Americans need to understand that before *The Help* and *Driving Miss Daisy* of the '40s, '50s and '60s, there were the helpers and drivers of the Civil

War and post-Civil War. This is the heritage that our movie stars and entertainers should be embracing. They should help to restore this vital part of our people's history and not relegate it as a thing of the past never to be remembered. I finally came to embrace this when, out of curiosity, I visited the website of a local Sons of The Confederate Camp (#265) in Mississippi. I was amazed at what level of interest the camp dedicated to "Black Confederates." At that moment, I had a subconscious understanding that these people couldn't possibly be against Black folks. The information on their website gave me a sense of comfort in knowing that my history would be valued instead of rejected. I just had one more step to take. I had to go see for myself. So, I went to the local relic show sponsored by Camp #265 in Brandon, Mississippi. This trip helped me to elevate my research to confirm what I had known since 2008. My thoughts were clear. If a White guy in Rankin County, Mississippi, could value the roles of Blacks in the Civil War, then certainly I had every right to do the same and even more so. To value the service of men and women who have been written out of this historical narrative could only be an honor. They were men like Turner Hall, Jr., who helped the Confederacy fight a war that lasted for four long and brutal years. These were men who helped build a country through their sacrifice. Why not build into this historical narrative? How about a movie about them? I think it is quite hypocritical for actors and actresses to make millions of dollars from the stories that they choose to play on the big screen and then turn around and attempt to use their influence in ways that will destroy the history of what has brought them fame. We have only seen a glimpse of the role that African Americans played in the Civil War through the movie, *Glory*. I would love to see a movie on Blacks' role in the war on both sides of the battle. Maybe that wouldn't be the politically correct thing to see but it would be historically accurate, to say the least. What is it about truth that makes it so hard to accept? Is it because we, too, have allowed our history to be hijacked by a certain era? Has our own hatred and deep-rooted sin, anger, bitterness, and un-forgiveness caused us to blot out our own historical records? That's exactly what we are doing when we take the Confederate flag out of its entire context and make it a symbol of hate and racism. Ignorance can no longer be our way forward. For the sake of history and to honor the thousands of former slaves who served under the Confederate flag, I can't succumb to ignorance. History, the good, bad, and the ugly, is important.

Frederick Douglass stated of the Negroes in the South:

> Frederick Douglass, Douglass' Monthly, IV [Sept. 1861], pp. 516: "there are at the present moment many colored men in the Confederate Army—as real soldiers, having muskets on their shoulders, and

bullets in their pockets, ready to shoot down loyal troops, and do all that soldiers may do to destroy the Federal government. [. . .] There were such soldiers at Manassas and they are probably there still." ("Negroes in the Confederate Army," Journal of Negro History, Charles Wesle, Vol. 4, #3, [1919], 244–245)

Frederick Douglass stated of the Negroes in the North:

"The true history of this war will show that the loyal army found no friends at the South so faithful, active, and daring in their efforts to sustain the Government as the Negroes. It will be shown that they have been the safest guides to our army and the best pilots to our navy, and the most dutiful laborers on our fortifications, where they have been permitted thus to serve. It is already known that the tremendous slaughter of loyal soldiers at Pittsburgh Landing, where our army was surprised and cut to pieces, would have been prevented had the alarm given by a Negro, who had risked his life to give it, [had] been taken. The same is true of the destruction of the Maryland Regiment the other day at Port Royal. Gen. Burnside, in the difficult task committed to him of feeling his way into the intricate rivers and creeks of Virginia and North Carolina, had found no assistance among the so-called loyal whites comparable in value to that obtained from intelligent Black men. The folly and expense of marching an army to Manassas, after it had been evacuated more than a week, would have been prevented but for the contemptuous disregard of information conveyed by the despised men of color. Negroes have repeatedly threaded their way through the lines of the rebels exposing themselves to bullets to convey important information to the loyal army of the Potomac. Thousands of lives and millions of treasure might have been saved to the Government if these services had been appreciated by Commanding Generals. It was a Negro who struck the first terrible blow at rebel privatizing by killing the pirates and capturing the vessel, and today there is no man of the same opportunity so serviceable to the loyal army in South Carolina, as Robert Smalls, the colored pilot. The whites of the South, rich and poor, receive the loyal soldiers with sullen aversion, who the Blacks deem it their highest privilege to do them a service, although for doing so they have been delivered up by ungrateful officers to their rebel masters to suffer stripes and death. They seem determined to deserve credit whether they get it or not." (Fredrick Douglass, 1818–1895)

Frederick Douglass lays claim to the reality that Black men and slaves were not sitting idle with their arms folded watching White men fight. Slaves and free men of color were actively engaged in the Civil War on both sides and in many capacities. It is a mistake to think that there were not free men of color fighting in the Confederate army. This is the reality that I have come to accept. It is a reality that still awaits millions of modern African Americans.

NATHAN BEDFORD FORREST: THE GOOD, BAD & THE UGLY

General Nathan Bedford Forrest was the first grand wizard of the KKK. General Ulysses Grant called him, "that devil Forrest." It is noted that Tecumseh Sherman said of him, "The most remarkable man our Civil War produced on either side." At the end of the war, General Robert E. Lee was asked who was his best general. His reply, "That honor belongs to a general I have never met, Nathan Bedford Forrest." No other name would strike fear in the heart of Union commanders more than his name. No one name would bring hope to the hearts of Confederates on the battle field more than his name.

I will never forget the day I discovered my great-great-grandfather was owned by the family firm of Nathan Bedford Forrest. Because of my study of the Civil War and my quest to find out more about my ancestor's role as an orderly, I knew my generals on both sides of the conflict. Forrest was the one general that I didn't like. One of the things he was remembered for during the war was the Fort Pillow Massacre in Tennessee. Hundreds of Black soldiers and White officers were slaughtered after attempting to surrender. The term "no quarters" was heard on the battleground to signify the command to not take prisoners. It is debated among historians if Forrest had anything to do with the slaughter. Many Southerners, in order to protect his integrity, choose to deny that he had any responsibility for the killings. It is often said that his subordinates got out of control. The Fort Pillow Massacre has been a blemish on Forrest's military record since the war and even today is a highly contested issue. It is still an issue of controversy today. I personally think that Forrest was such a great general; he would have accepted full responsibility for any atrocities under his command. He wasn't a coward and didn't need defending on the battlefield. Because of this issue and his brief association with the KKK, his image has suffered. I have named him the Twisted General. If I may, I will use modern Black slang to convey what I think has happened. It's the phrase, "Don't get it twisted."

I do believe Forrest has been twisted. On the one hand, he is given too much moral grace; and on the other hand, given way too much evil indignation. The Civil War was a blood bath on many fronts. Like all humans, and he was human, many experiences are responsible for making us who we are. Not just the good ones, but the bad ones as well. Before I go into the twist of Forrest, let me tell you of my own. . . .

Talking about a twist. I cannot tell you how twisted I was when I got the information from the Oklahoma Historical Society leading me to the knowledge that Nathan Bedford Forrest owned my great-great-grandfather. I was totally knocked down. He was the one Southern general that I had not warmed up to in all of my studies of the Civil War. Largely, the Fort

Pillow Massacre had skewed my impression of the general. My eldest son attends Belmont University in Nashville, Tennessee. On visits to see him, I had refused to even look at the statue of Nathan Bedford Forrest on the interstate leading into the city of Nashville.

In preparation for our 15th annual Memorial Day weekend family reunion in Monroe County, Mississippi, I was doing family research on my ancestor, hoping to obtain new information. I was also preparing to share information on my ancestor at a local Sons of The Confederate Civil War relic show in June. The relic show, hosted by the Rankin Rough and Readys Camp #265 in Rankin County, Mississippi, is widely attended. My mind was twisted, indeed. I knew of my ancestor's possible connection to General Lee. I also very well knew that he had not run away to the North or to join the Union. I knew that he had gone to the Gettysburg Black Diamond Reunion in 1938 as a Confederate representative. But, I had settled my mind, heart, and thoughts with these facts. This issue of being owned by Forrest—and the fact that he was still cherishing, at the age of ninety-five, the Confederate money given to him by Forrest—was just overwhelming.

I knew Forrest was a great general. I also knew of his association with the KKK. My uncles and relatives who grew up in the '50s and '60s, when the Klan was notorious against Blacks, would be present at the annual family reunion. I have strong nerves, but I wanted to shrink back from this one. I could see myself being burned at the stake at the family reunion in May and being hailed a hero at the Confederate show in June. How could this be?

I could not deny what was printed in the local *Oklahoman* on November 25, 1937. I read it over and over and over. And as they say in the South, "I'll be damn if it didn't say Nathan Bedford Forrest."

I ran outside with chills over my body. I laughed and then I said, "Oh crap, this is crap!" I sat down again and read it again. It was no mistake. I had a *Good Times* Flo moment. "DAMN, DAMN, DAMN, FORREST!" (African Americans remember that day and know what I am talking about. It was the day the father of the family, James, died on the 1970s hit series, *Good-Times.*)

There he stood, my great-great-grandfather flanked between two young sons of the Confederate at ninety-five years old. A photo that no one in my family had ever laid eyes on. I didn't know whether to laugh or cry but I had to make up my mind soon. The family reunion and the Confederate relic show were right around the corner. I had to prepare to tell my huge family that the family firm of Nathan Bedford Forrest, a historical notorious figure, owned our ancestor. But if that was true, I had to know more about Forrest the man. Perhaps it would give me some insight into the mind of my ancestor. One thing about this new information that was clear to me was that my ancestor admired and cherished General Forrest.

After doing my homework on Forrest, this is what I have concluded, and this is what I conveyed to my family. General Nathan Bedford Forrest was like the one White boy back in the neighborhood that really could jump. You know, the one we grew up with that all the brothers were friends with because, at the end of the day, he could whip your butt. The Larry Bird of basketball. All the brothers in my neighborhood loved the Lakers and the 76ers. Magic Johnson and Julius Irving (Dr. J) were doing some new things on the court that young Black boys dreamed of doing. However, there was still one dirty White boy always standing in the way. Larry Bird was that man on the court.

I was the only Boston Celtics fan on the school bus. We had multiple backyard stadiums in the neighborhood. Who won the last game on TV determined where we played the next sand-lock match. My Boston Garden was the host of many great games. I took the risk and it gave me plenty of bragging rights. Every Black person knows of at least one of these White boys. It's just better to be down with him because he is a beast. He could do stuff that no White boy was supposed to be able to do.

I remember playing football at Shannon High School. One of our rivalry teams, Pontotoc, had one of these White boys in the back field. The scouting report was clear. One man couldn't take him and whatever you do, please don't hit him low. Well, I took the risk and got pummeled as Wesley Walls' cleats literally went over my facemask as he entered the end zone. Walls went on to have a stellar Pro Bowl career in the NFL. I saw him once hit a baseball straight up in the air and when the ball landed it was behind the center-field wall on the football practice field. It was a home run!

Well, Forrest only struck twice! One bad strike on the battlefield and one bad strike off the battlefield. Some would give him a third strike for his post-war activities. I don't. As painful as it is, history does not allow us to strip things out of context. If we do that, we might as well destroy the whole of humanity for the depravity that has existed from the fall of man. Everything else that Forrest did was a home run. Put that in perspective and you can maybe realize why he is so respected over one hundred and fifty years later.

Forrest was the one general in the neighborhood that you didn't want to run into on the battlefield. Out of fifty-four battles, he only lost one. He had twenty-nine horses shot from under him during the war. He was wounded eight times. He had no formal military training but his tactics are still studied today. He was just a backyard home-trained rebel who fought with a purpose. Destroy the enemy!

His maneuvers at The Battle of Brice's Crossroads are regarded by some military historians as the single best military maneuvering of any general in the history of our country. William Tecumseh Sherman said it best, "War is Hell." Anything other than that perception of war is not reality. Fort Pillow I have studied from both sides of the argument. I have concluded that Blacks were there. They were there on both sides of the battle. Unfortunately, many do not realize that Forrest had Blacks with him at this battle. At the end of the day, it was pure hell. But that is war. It brings me more validity to say that this is the very reason why Blacks, regardless of what side of the war they were on, should be commended. Any man who is brave enough to take up arms and fight, or brave enough to stand behind those who take up arms and fight, is worthy of the respect and honor that only a war can produce. When and if on the battlefield the decision to kill or be killed is made, who am I to second-guess the thought of a man in the heat of a war? Even those who say it was a matter of policy before the battle to take "no quarters" for Blacks, policy doesn't read well when musket balls are flying high over your head. Needless to say, this is not the only example of such acts during the Civil War. A similar plight happened to Blacks at The Battle of Saltville, Virginia, when dozens of Black soldiers were dragged out of a hospital and killed.

People today talk about Forrest and Fort Pillow as if it was the only act that could have been considered a war crime. The Union army was just as guilty of potential war crimes. Sherman's march on Atlanta saw the brutal treatment of Black slave women by his Union soldiers. After all, it was Sherman who said, "War is Hell." What do you think the Northern general did when he saw these atrocities? Absolutely nothing.

In Osceola, Missouri, a pro-abolitionist political general, Senator James Lane, had nine military-age Southern men shot and killed for nothing other than they were suspected of aiding the Confederacy. What African Americans today need to understand is that slaves did whatever they could to survive and they caught hell doing it on both sides of the war. Yet, their bravery, chivalry, ingenuity, loyalty, and faith in God brought many through their trials.

There are other aspects of Forrest's character not known by many African Americans. One is that he is noted to be the first Southern White man to kiss Black women in public. He also has historically been known as one of the first White civil rights advocates. He was the first White man to be invited to speak before an all-Black pre-NAACP convention in 1875. Kissing Black women during the era of slavery certainly wasn't against the law. But to do so in public was not the acceptable norm. One of the worst whippings of the Civil War era was a pre-war beating of a radical Republican Senator by a Southern Senator from South Carolina, Preston Brooks. An undercurrent behind this beating was centered on sexual overtones by both sides indicating relationships with Black women. The political rhetoric of the day included strong accusations of sexual exploitation. Southern gentlemen accused abolitionist of promoting interracial relationships. Radicals accused Southern gentleman of wanting to protect slavery to protect their sexual exploitation of slave women. Sumner's speech on the Senate floor was laden with sexual overtones.

> "The Senator from South Carolina has read many books of chivalry, and believes himself a chivalrous knight with sentiments of honor and courage. Of course he has chosen a mistress to whom he has made his vows, and who, though ugly to others, is always lovely to him; though polluted in the sight of the world, is chaste in his sight—I mean the harlot, slavery. For her his tongue is always profuse in words. Let her be impeached in character, or any proposition made to shut her out from the extension of her wantonness, and no extravagance of manner or hardihood of assertion is then too great for this Senator." (Charles Sumner, May 25, 1856)

Forrest's gesture of embracing a Black woman in public was certainly not the norm of the day. But Forrest was no normal Civil War General. He was not a military school General nor was he a political General. He was an uneducated, blue collar General, if you will. Nathan Bedford Forrest was a full man and a real warrior. Not a soft bone in his body and especially on the battlefield. Forrest, on July 5, 1875, embraced this Black woman at an organized event sponsored by The Independent Order of Pole-Bearers Association. This organization was the predecessor to the NAACP.

> "Ladies and Gentlemen, I accept the flowers as a memento of reconciliation between the white and colored races of the Southern states. I accept it more particularly as it comes from a colored lady, for if there is any one on God's earth who loves the ladies I believe it is myself. (Immense applause and laughter.) I came here with the jeers of some white people, who think that I am doing wrong. I believe I can exert some influence, and do much to assist the people in strengthening fraternal relations, and shall do all in my power to elevate every man to depress none. I want to elevate you to take positions in law offices, in stores, on farms, and wherever you are capable of going. I have not said anything about politics today. I don't propose to say anything about politics. You have a right to elect whom you please; vote for the man you think best, and I think, when that is done, you and I are freemen. Do as you consider right and hones in electing men for office. I did not come here to make you a long speech, although invited to do so by yours. I am not much of a speaker, and my business prevented me from preparing myself. I came to meet you as friends, and welcome you to the white people. I want you to come nearer to us. When I can serve you, I will do so. We have but one flag, one country; let us stand together. We may differ in color, but not in sentiment [. . .] many things have been said about

me which are wrong, and which white and black persons here, who stood by me through the war, can contradict. Go to work, be industrious, live honestly, and act truly, and when you are oppressed I'll come to your relief. I thank you, ladies and gentlemen, for this opportunity you have afforded me to be wit you, and assure you that I am with you in heart and in hand. (Prolonged applause.) (General Nathan Bedford Forrest, July 5, 1875)

Whereupon, Nathan Bedford Forrest again thanked Miss Lewis for the bouquet and then gave her a kiss on the cheek. Such a kiss was unheard of in the society of those days, in 1875, but it showed a token of respect and friendship between the general and the Black community and did much to promote harmony among the citizens of Memphis. (Tennessee-SCV.org)

General Forrest was also a man who evoked deep loyalty from his slaves. When the war started, General Forrest took forty-five slaves with him to battle. At the end of the war, all but one stood with him. It is reported that he informed the slaves at the onset that they would be fighting for their freedom. If the South lost, they would be set free. If the South won the war, he would set them free. Either way, they would be free. Forrest bestowed honor upon these men as among the bravest Confederate soldiers as any in his camp. Furthermore, it is noted that in his handpicked inner circle of the best Calvary men that he possessed, at least eight were slaves.

"I said to 45 colored fellows on my plantation that I was going into the army; and if they would go with me, if we got whipped they would be free anyhow, and that if we succeeded and slaver was perpetrated, if they would act faithfully with me to the end of the war, I would set them free. Eighteen months before the war closed I was satisfied that we were going to be defeated, and I have those 45, or 44 of them, their free papers for fear I might be called." (General Nathan Bedford Forrest, Congressional Testimony after the war).

In late August of 1868, General Nathan Bedford Forrest gave an interview to a reporter. Forrest said of the Black men who served with him: "These boys stayed with me…and better Confederates did not live." (Forrest, 1868)

Black Private Louis Napoleon Nelson served the Confederate states of America at Shiloh, Lookout Mountain, Brice's Crossroads and Vicksburg as soldier and chaplain in the 7th Tennessee Cavalry, under Lt. General Nathan Bedford Forrest.

Col. Parkhurts's (Northern) Account of Forrest's Black Confederates:

The forces attacking my camp were the First Regiment Texas Rangers, a battalion of the First Georgia Rangers . . . and quite a number of Negroes attached to the Texas and Georgia troops, who were armed and equipped and took part in the several engagements with my forces during the day."

(Lieutenant Colonel Parkhurst's Report, Ninth Michigan Infantry, on General Forrest's attack at Murfreesboro, Tennessee, July 13, 1862, in official Records, Series I, Vol XVI, Part I, page 805)

GOD'S SALVATION

It came in the fall of 1875 prior to Forrest's presentation at the Independent Order of Pole-Bearers Association meeting. Reverend George Tucker Stainback preached from these Holy Words:

> "Everyone then who hears these words of mine and does them will be like a wise man who built his house on the rock. And the rain fell, and the floods came, and the winds blew and beat on that house, but it did not fall, because it had been founded on the rock. And everyone who hears these words of mine and does not do them will be like a foolish man who built his house on the sand. And the rain fell, and the floods came, and the winds blew and beat against that house, and it fell, and great was the fall of it." (Matthew 7:24–27)

In the pews that day was Nathan Bedford Forrest. According to Rev. Stainback, Forrest said to him, "Sir, your sermon has removed the last prop from under me. I am the fool that built on the sand. I am a poor miserable sinner."

The Reverend gave Forrest the challenge of reading these words in the privacy of his home:

> "Have mercy on me, O God, according to your steadfast love; according to your abundant mercy blot out my transgressions. Wash me thoroughly from my iniquity, and cleanse me from my sin! For I know my transgressions, and my sin is ever before me." (Psalm 51:1–3)

The preacher followed up with Forrest the next day and they prayed together as Forrest accepted his Redeemer. On his dying bed, two years latter, Forrest said, "There is no cloud that separates me from my Heavenly Father."

What God-fearing Christian man or women today would deny that God's salvation did not come to Nathan Bedford Forrest on that fall day in 1875? If any Christian declares that this is not salvation, as we know the scriptures to teach, then he stands to be judged as the man who built his house upon sand. If you say this is not a biblical understanding of faith in Christ by Grace, you are standing in your own salvation and not that of God. The beauty of salvation is in God, not the sinner. How beautifully did he call this dear brother to Himself through His preached Word! He shall call all of His children to this marvelous light. And they will be redeemed for His glory.

Any man who denies God's salvation of Nathan Bedford Forrest and refuses to allow this great military general and redeemed soul to rest in peace and with honor must also deny all of John Newton's hymn, *Amazing Grace*, and all of the writings of Apostle Paul. Newton was a slave trader of the most serious kind. Apostle Paul persecuted Christians to the point of death. They both heard a cry from heaven by the same Holy Spirit that saved Nathan Bedford Forrest. Like Forrest, scales fell from their eyes. They realized that they, too, were standing on sand. They repented of their sins and we now enjoy the wonderful blessings of God's redemption of these two souls. It is time for Black Christians to acknowledge the same grace for Forrest or forever cease to sing the great Christian hymn written by a former slave trader. To deny this hymn in our worship of God would fundamentally change the Black church forever. There is not one African-American Church in this country that doesn't know this great hymn was given to us, the body of Christ, by a former slave trader. How ironic, the president of these great United States and our African-American political hero led the Church in South Carolina in song by using the hymn of John Newton, a former slaver. This hymn was a main source of comfort and unifying force among Blacks and Whites attending the funeral of Pastor Clementa Pinckney. All of America, if not the world, witnessed triumph over evil, hatred and sin through this song. How is it that we can afford forgiveness to this brother, Newton, and not extend it to our brother Forrest? Do we have scales on our eyes? Was Newton any less of a sinner than Forrest? Was Apostle Paul? No! These men were no more sinner than any man! Yet, like Apostle Paul, Forrest claimed himself to be the worst of sinners.

Therefore, are we to deny the writings of the great Apostle Paul? God forbid! This is why I now gaze upon the Nashville statue of Forrest with tears in my eyes. I rest upon a monument and testimony to the great Grace of God. This is what Turner Hall, Jr. knew and understood about grace. This is why, seventy-two years after the Civil War, he could be found professing possessions given to him by General Forrest as his most prized. For he, too, was a sinner saved by this same marvelous grace. It also speaks to how he must have thought about Forrest even during the war. May Forrest remembrance, like that of John Newton and Apostle Paul, forever challenge us of our own sin and remind us what is ours through faith in Christ, our great and Almighty God. If the Black and White folks who think Forrest's and other Civil War monuments are to be destroyed, it is because they don't rightly see grace or the value of honoring and remembering the greatness of these generals and their value to history, both good and bad. Give me the remains of the greatest military general in the history of our country, Nathan Bedford Forrest, and I will build a monument in the heart of downtown Jackson, Mississippi and revitalize a dilapidated community by establishing the largest Civil War museum in this country. We could use the proceeds from such site to restore this community. We could educate our children on our past so that they learn factual truths about history and what role our people played in it. In fact, Jackson, Mississippi has enough Civil war history and Black history of that era to underwrite the best paved streets in the country. Yet, we rather settle on our elderly poor paying high water bills and taxes to patch our roads. We pat ourselves on the back as if we are progressing. As we say in the great state of Mississippi: "Hogwash." We don't look to build on our rich history to attract people from all over the world to see. We put our heads in the holes of history and continue to cripple our people with ignorance. Instead of using our history to unite us, we fall into the trap of an unforgiving spirit and a bitterness that separate us from our rich history and valuable resources.

Finally, back to that Confederate money. In my mind, there are three possibilities to explain how my ancestor had Confederate money given to him by General Forrest. Confederate monies were issued between 1861-1865. The first possibility that I had to consider was that it could have been given to him for his service as one of Forrest's forty-five slaves who served with him. I don't hold to this first possibility for two reasons. First, I found no documentation to support that he was numbered among the forty-five slaves whom Forrest took to war with him. Another reason is that it is documented that he served as a body servant for two non-commissioned Confederate soldiers. The second possibility was that General Forrest could have presented Turner, Jr. with the Confederate money after the war. I don't find anything that states that this didn't happen, but it just doesn't seem plausible considering the money at that point was worthless. However, if this second possibility is correct, it would take on more meaning, signifying an even deeper relationship among the two men. It would be similar to two old friends getting together for a beer after a long hard struggle and one giving the other a keepsake as a token of something to be remembered for the good ol' times. Although this view is very possible, I tend to lean to the third alternative. The money was given to him as part of a dynamic relationship that had been forged between the slave master and the slave. If you take into account that Bedford Forrest took forty-five of his slaves with him at the onset of the war (and I don't consider my great-great grandfather to be one of them) then it is my estimate that he would have been owned by Forrest before the war started. Moreover, Forrest had a reputation of being kind toward his slaves and taking good care of them. This leads me to believe that during his role as a body servant for two Confederate soldiers, he would have come into contact with his former master and obtained this monetary gift during the war in passing between a former master and slave. Taking into account that General Robert E. Lee and General Forrest never met during the war, this opens up the idea that Turner would have traveled with his Confederate comrades throughout the theater of the war and at some point been introduced to General Robert E.

Lee. At that point, he would have assumed duties of caretaker for Lee's horse Traveller among other things based upon a recommendation. I gather he was likely introduced to Lee as "one of Bedford's slaves." If you consider Lee's admiration for Bedford Forrest, Bedford's reputation of having very loyal slaves as a result of being a good master, as well as Turner's prior superb service to two Confederate soldiers, a recommendation to General Lee would have been all he needed to gain clearance to be numbered worthy as one of General Lee's servants.

I am convinced now more than ever that Turner Hall, Jr. and Nathan Bedford Forrest are in the same heaven. They have now, at this moment, more friendship than they ever could have had on earth. How sweet would it be if the descendants from their generation could abide in the same love. Only in Christ are we able to see that their lives and their history affords us this wonderful opportunity

THE BLACK CONFEDERATE, TURNER HALL, JR.

Route 1, Box 207-A
Pierce City, MO 65723
March 20, 1983

"Mr. R. E. Jackson of Aberdeen, Mississippi has suggested that I write to you for information regarding <u>Turner Hall</u> who died in 1942.

Let me introduce myself and explain the reason for this long letter. I am now a retired government worker from Washington, D.C. I have been a writer all my life and now write about six magazine articles a year. When I was graduated from school in 1938, one of my first jobs was editor of the daily newspaper at Hugo, Oklahoma. It was there that I first met <u>Turner Hall</u> who at that time was a fine old man who was nearly 100 years old who liked to talk about General Lee and how he, Turner Hall, took care of the General's horse, Traveler. I remember that he went to New York City in April, 1940, and was interviewed on the CBS nationwide radio show "We, the People."

In the autumn of 1940 I left Hugo to enter the military service. In 1980, some 40 years later, the editor of a children's magazine was interested in a story about Black history, and I suggested the Turner Hall story. Needless to say, I have never written the story because I have been unable to gather the necessary information for it. After a 40-year absence I returned to Hugo and found that the old generation was gone and the new generation knew little or nothing about the pre-World War II period. The old newspaper files had been destroyed and the CBS network headquarters in New York City reported that the transcript of Turner Hall's interview was not available. I began a search for (type faded) but did not know where to start. I could not find any funeral home in Hugo, and I had no idea in what year Turner Hall died. I searched the cemeteries for a grave marker, with no success. So many of the graves"....... 2nd page of letter lost. (Mystery Writer, letter to family, March 20, 1983)

For years it remained a mystery letter. Placed in our family heritage book with the caption, "A letter to Sammie Hall, Sr., with someone searching for information about Turner Hall." The family lost the second page of the letter dated March 20, 1983, from Pierce City, Missouri. This mystery writer was inquiring about the final whereabouts of Turner Hall. It wasn't until 2014 that I discovered the name of the writer. I decided to attend a local Civil War relic show hosted by the SCV Camp #265 in Rankin County, Mississippi. The Sons of Confederate Veterans camp was known as the "Rough and Ready's" in Brandon, Mississippi.

This would be my first time to be brave enough to snoop around the doorstep of my Confederacy. I wanted to gauge the degree of my reception or rejection of my fellow Confederate brethren. To my dismay, my time was filled with sincere welcomes and open doors. Southern hospitality was on full display. I was also shocked at how engaging the participants were regarding issues of slavery, Blacks in the Civil War, and the historical record of their service. I even had one Black family come to my table to discuss how I found information on my ancestor.

I had no idea this first-time visit to a Civil War relic show would close a vital gap in our family history. I would discover the name of the mystery writer. One of my purchases on that day was a book, *Black Confederates* (Barrow, Seagars & Rosenburg). I was casually reading the book in my spare time one day and I finally came to page 74. I couldn't believe my eyes. There was a paragraph making reference to Turner Hall, my ancestor.

> "Turner Hall, II, born October 11, 1842, in North Carolina, often told stories of his servant days in the war. He seldom failed to speak of his having been an orderly for Gen. Robert E. Lee (possibly so, but unverified). He was brought to Hugo, Oklahoma, by Judge Trice from Mississippi in 1906. Hall went to the Diamond Battle Reunion at Gettysburg in 1938 and later appeared on "We, the people" radio show in New York City. Widely respected by all who knew him, he was buried (according to Otis E. Hays, Jr., of

Pierce City, Missouri) near Nettleton, Mississippi."
(Jay S. Hoar, *The South's Last Boys in Gray*, 18)

Not only did we learn that he was named after his father but we also learned that he was a very traveled man. Pennsylvania, New York City! Turner Hall, Jr. was born a slave in North Carolina in 1840 (not in Rankin County, North Carolina, as one article suggests; there is no Rankin County in North Carolina). We believed he died in 1948. His burial place remains unknown. In the buying and selling of slaves, my great-great-grandfather found himself in Mississippi. I am not sure of the transactions that led to his departure from North Carolina. However, we are certain that he must have been separated from his immediate family. Our family history reveals no record that his father, my great-great-great-grandfather, Turner Hall, Sr. ever left North Carolina. In honor of Turner Hall, Sr. from this point forward, I refer to my great-great-grandfather as Turner, Jr. It's a way to remind me that he had a dad whom I'm sure loved him very much.

A young slave boy: Through research, it is revealed to us that at some point in his youth he found himself among the property holdings of one of the most revered Confederate families, "The Family firm of Nathan Bedford Forrest." For the record, the Forrest firm was a very successful and large slave-trading company. After the war, the Forrests made huge profits by working ex-slaves in the penal system throughout the South.

However, Turner, Jr., was among the former dealings of the Forrest family personal slave plantation, instead of his penal operations. It is believed based upon a 1937 newspaper article that his appreciation for Nathan Bedford Forest was one that would have developed over time. He portrayed a kind of expressed appreciation that a faithful and loyal slave would have had for a faithful master in his day.

Not many African Americans know or even care to know who owned their ancestors. Slavery is a thing of the past and the difficulty of Blacks as property and not as people hinders the efforts that most African Americans would like to take to find out more about their ancestry. My first introduction to family genealogy came at the expense of my dear wife. It occurred at a family reunion, one of her first gatherings with my family. Thanks to cousin Troy Lee's having one too many beers, genealogy became a source of laughter for some time. Cousin Troy Lee, an older relative in the family, saw her getting out of the car and was so struck by her beauty he exclaimed in a full drunken voice, "A full-blooded Choctaw! Come here babe! I got full-blood Cherokee in my veins!" He picked her up off her feet and gave her a bear hug and a kiss before I could get around the vehicle to save her from her despair. Needless to say, she kept an eye out for ol' Troy Lee for the next two family reunions. I knew my wife wasn't a Choctaw and Troy Lee was the blackest Cherokee I had ever seen if there were any truth to his claim.

The fact that we are uniquely referred to as African Americans speaks volumes to the reality that we, Blacks in America, are inherently linked to the motherland, Africa. Indeed, we were brought to this country as slaves. I just happen to be one of those who cares enough about that link and all that it represents. I dared to research the depths of what it means to me. I was given a window of opportunity to find out more about my ancestors through this one ancestor, Turner Hall.

A young man—Confederate flunkie: At the start of the Civil War, Turner, Jr. was between nineteen and twenty-one years old. Family research shows he served as a "body servant" for two Confederate soldiers and there is one reference to him as an "orderly" for Robert E. Lee (although unverified). Being a flunky, orderly, or servant for Confederate soldiers was routine duty for many enslaved men of his age. Although it must be known that these men would have fought, if needed.

I am not one who contends that large-scale slaves were incorporated as soldiers in the Confederacy. I am one to contend that thousands of slaves served the Confederacy in various capacities. Some did serve as soldiers. This fact is evident based upon the pension records and multiple historical accounts that can easily be found with proper research. Both sides of the war were officially reluctant to employ slaves or free Blacks as soldiers. By the end of the war, both sides had changed their minds in this regard. There is nothing in the historical record that we can find that my great-great-grandfather's role as a servant in the Confederate army and orderly for General Lee was ever disputed. He lived during a time when many ex-Confederates lived and not once do we find any dispute of his claim to have served faithfully throughout the war. I think one reason we find no dispute is that his words, like most men of his day, were truthful words. It's certainly hard for a modern man to come to grips with the reality that there once was a time when a man's word was his bond. He did not speak unless he spoke with honor and truth.

As far as his capacity as a flunky or orderly, not much is specifically recorded about the duties of such individuals other than what is commonly known. They did whatever was needed to assist those they served. The fact that many Blacks were written out of the history by writers who took no interest in the roles of Blacks doesn't mean that they didn't have roles. In fact, it is widely known that had it not been for the flunkies, orderlies, and servants who labored for the Confederacy, their fight would have not been as productive as it was on many fronts. The home front of the Southerners alone would have virtually collapsed had it not been for the slaves carrying on their duty. After all, Southern men went to fight while their women and children were left to attend the home front. Fortunately, for some former slaves, verification is possible through pension records.

Unfortunately, for far too many Black Confederate servants, it is impossible to verify their service to the Confederacy.

What is clear to our family is that Turner Hall Jr. not only started the war with the Confederacy, he ended the war with the Confederacy and was very proud of it. Moreover, one must ask himself today what the circumstances were that would have led a slave to serve beside Confederate soldiers? All too common is the notion that they served because they had to. Although that may have been the circumstances for some it is not that black and white. Some served because they got paid as cooks and for other tasks in the army. That would have been a tangible way for them to provide for their families. Inflationary costs were extremely high during the Civil War just like in any war. Many had never left their communities or states, and it was unrealistic at that time to venture the risk of life with family that could have included small children or elders. Another circumstance would have been enduring relationships developed between body servants and those they served. Contrary to our modern thought of what we would have done or thought, these people were real people who developed real lasting relationships even across racial lines.

A man (and loyal servant): At the age of twenty-three the war had ended for Turner, Jr. Boys go off to war and they come back men. What of the slave? Was he not subject to the same toils of war, if not worse? His plight was intimately tied to the plight of his masters. From those days in 1861–1865 to this day, bullets and cannon balls with all of their gore has never been known to have eyes. Considering that the Civil War has been one of the bloodiest wars our nation has ever endured, I wonder how many times he was almost killed? Do people really think that Black men were sitting under the shade trees watching White men fight? If so, that's a wrong perception of what actually happened. I can assure you that when the Black men heard the roar of the cannon, he ducked just as the White man beside him. At the same time, when men were called to fight, Black men also took it upon themselves to fight. Again, I do not contend that there was wholesale use of Black men fighting with arms for the Confederacy, or even the Union for that matter. However, the historical record of Blacks during times of war is clear. Black men have had a role in every war in the history of this country dating back to the Revolutionary War.

I cannot devalue the role of Turner, Jr. in the Confederate army. To do so, would be to undermine his character and the character of the thousands of other servants and even Black Confederate soldiers who fought and died during a war that was epic. There has always been a dispute about the value, role, or capacity of Black men's involvement in wars. Even today, in 2015, at the writing of this manuscript, a posthumous award, the highest military award, was given to a Black soldier, Pvt. Henry Johnson, for his bravery in World War I in 1918, an act that was well recorded and known by his superiors but written out of history because of his race. Forgotten! How about the fact that he is just now being remembered ninety-seven years later? I will not forget Turner, Jr. I will remember him and the flag that he honored. One hundred and fifty years later after the war, I will tell his story.

Look at this way. It is only forty-nine years between the end of the Civil War and the start of World War I. That short span of fifty years didn't see much improvement in the equality of African Americans in military ranks. In fact, many African Americans were turned away for military service during World War I despite their willingness and ability to serve. African Americans had proved themselves in the Indian Wars and the Spanish-American Wars. The famous Buffalo Soldiers were formed just one year after the end of the Civil War in 1866. When you put things in perspective, the proximity of these wars is very close and the continuity of service of African Americans has been consistent throughout history. Thus, I don't have to agree with all that the Confederacy represents in order to hold it in high esteem. I choose to honor my ancestor from a historical perspective and that is the focus of Confederate heritage.

On the other hand, I don't have to tear down the history of the Confederacy or forget it all together. Turner, Jr. didn't do that, and I can't allow the hijacking of the Confederacy in my generation and the previous generation to destroy the historical implications that he shared with many African-American men, though they were slaves at the time. They were men of their time. It is improper to take your existing time span and historical perspective and apply it to the lens of time and history by removing the original historical context. Applying a new historical context to a previous time period is simply wrong. Men who used the Confederate flag to portray supremacist views and bigotry brought the flag of the Confederacy back into use during the civil rights era. The battle flag of the Confederate army had not flown since the end of the war in 1865.

I often wonder about the first Confederate soldier that he served. What happened to him? Was he killed? Did he get wounded? If so, did he return home? If so, why in the hell didn't my great-great-grandfather go home with him? He would stay until the end. Was the second Confederate soldier a friend of the first? I can assume they very well could have been boyhood companions of Turner, Jr. That was often the pattern. Because there are virtually no records on slaves in the war at that time, these are questions that perhaps I will never know the answer. Yet, there is one thing I am certain. Turner, Jr. was loyal. Call him what you will. During the war several terms were used for servants. They were called flunkies, slaves, contraband, body servants, and orderlies. I am OK with these terms. I don't marvel at the terms. He was a man of Confederate conviction and a man with a sense of purpose. And that is what I marvel at.

Did he have options? I'm almost certain he did. Perhaps his options weren't as grand as the modern Black man would like to think they would have been. Perhaps he considered choosing to run north or to join the Union. The fact remains, he didn't do either. He finished the course of the war as a Confederate orderly and returned to Mississippi after the war.

A family man, Turner, Jr. married Francis Dilworth on January 12th, 1876. They were married in Monroe County, Mississippi. By this time, he had worked for a prominent family in Okolona, Mississippi, for ten years. He worked for the Walton family in the neighboring county of Chickasaw. From 1879–1898 nine children were born to this union. His last daughter, Willie L. Hall, born March 27, 1898, was my great-grandmother.

Turner, Jr. was a very loyal man. Mr. Walton died and his wife, Mary, married into another prominent family in Okolona. She married Colonel Trice. Turner, Jr. served this Walton family line for four generations. When Mrs. Trice decided to move the family to Oklahoma, Turner, Jr. went with the family. They arrived in Hugo, Oklahoma, in 1906. He would care for one more generation of Walton's in Oklahoma. To this day, we still have relatives spread throughout Oklahoma.

"Aged Negro Serving Fifth In One Line"
Hugo Man Knew Lee in Civil War.

"Hugo, Nov. 24- (Special)- Turner Hall, 95 –year –old Hugo Negro, is serving the fifth generation of Waltons by assisting in the care of Charles Thomas and Billie Walton. Besides washing dishes, keeping the yard and bringing in wood at the J. O. Walton home.

Hall was born in 1842 in Ranking county, North Carolina, and at an early age "belonged to the family firm" of Gen. Nathan B. Forrest and Colonel Chambers.

He flunkied for the two Confederates during the Civil war and he saw Gen. Robert E. Lee "lots of times." He still cherishes Confederate money given to him by General Forrest."

After the Civil war, Hall went to live in the Bod Walton home at Okolona, Miss., and it was here that he began his first services for the first Walton, by taking Bob Walton's son, the late T. M. Walton to his first school.

When the late Jim Trice, brother-in-law to T. M. Walton, came to Oklahoma in 1903, Hall was brought along, coming to Hugo in the chartered railroad car with the Trice household goods and stock. He assisted in building the Trice home here on the present site of the new post-office building and Hall himself built his own little cabin in the rear, which was for many years a landmark. When the Trice property was sold to the government, Hall felt that he should be part of the deal, and only his advanced age kept him from being made janitor of the new building.

Turner has had a few outside interests which have made him a real part of a growing community and which have endeared him to the children.

He was a janitor for the First Baptist church for 15 years, of the Ross building for 13 years, and the First Presbyterian church for nearly 10 years.

His eyes are bright and clear, and though he had them tested for glasses some years back he doesn't use the glasses he bought. "I don't even put 'em in my pocket for I just used them to thread my needle," says the old man.

Hall spent July in Mississippi, having been given the trip by citizens. He visited scenes of his childhood. After the trip Hall feels that it is his duty to remain in Hugo, close by the Waltons' fireside and "watch out for" the family- the fourth and fifth generation of Waltons." *(The Daily Oklahoman*, Nov 25, 1937, The Oklahoma Historical Society)

I have secured seven newspaper articles on Turner, Jr., which have become historical artifacts for our family. We received five of these articles from the Oklahoma Historical Society in April of 2015. It was through these discoveries that we came to appreciate not only his loyalty to his Confederate service but his great appreciation for Nathan Bedford Forrest.

How ironic. The timing of the discovery was just two months away from the Charleston South Carolina church shooting that would reignite the battle over the Confederate flag; I was deep into my Confederate history. At least my family would have a historical perspective on the matter of the flag, Nathan Bedford Forrest, and Blacks in the Confederate army.

From the newspaper articles alone, we learned so much about Turner, Jr. He, for his time, was a well-traveled man. To this day, I can't lay claims that I have seen Washington DC or New York City. Since the election of our first African-American president, Washington DC has become the Mecca experience for Black folks. It's not about Washington DC as much as it is seeing Washington DC while Obama is still in office. That's the goal! That is what makes a trip to DC so sweet for many African Americans who have made this journey over the past seven years.

Turner, Jr. was well respected in his community. As a delegate, he received an all-expense-paid trip sponsored by a prominent company and citizens of the town of Hugo. We would come to find out that this would not be his only all-expense-paid trip. We are able to identify three separate trips that the citizens of Hugo gladly paid for him. The articles showed respect for Turner, Jr. was not only from White citizens but from Black citizens as well. The faithful and loyal servant was now being served.

When 1,000 veterans of the Blue and of the Gray bade one another sad farewells Tuesday and started home from Gettysburg, Pa., Hugo's delegates to the last reunion of Civil War Veterans, Turner Hall, and his escort James H. Milling, entrained for Washington, D. C., to "see the sights."

Mrs. Milling received a telegram from her husband Tuesday stating that they were in Washington and would probably arrive home Friday.

Like the other delegates, they report that they are having the time of their lives.

Meanwhile, trains pull out of Gettysburg carrying the veterans to their homes in all parts of the United States.

Departing for his St. Louis home, John M. Claypool, 92-year-old commander of the Confederate veterans, exulted:

"I've just been tickled to death. I've been to lots of reunions, but never anything like this. I knew it would be good, but it turned out better than anything I could conceive."

Claypool and Dr. Overton H. Mennett, G. A. R. commander, declared they had the "time of our lives."

About 1,000 veterans, half of those at the reunion, left for the west on the first two trains. The remainder start tomorrow.

Gettysburg folk, who enjoyed the veterans' visit perhaps more than did hundreds of thousands of sightseers, gathered at two branch line railroad depots to wave a last good-by.

Twenty-five veterans remained in the army camp hospital and nine others were being treated in hospitals in Gettysburg and nearby Carlisle. Most of the men needed only a rest but one, John W. Cooper, 91, of Largo, Fla., was reported in a critical condition from a heart attack. Most of the others would leave tomorrow, said Lieut. Col. Paul D. Hawley of the army medical corps.

"Hugo's Civil War Veteran and Escort Now In Washington, D.C."

"When 1,000 veterans of the Blue and of the Gray bade one another sad farewells Tuesday and started home from Gettysburg, Pa., Hugo's delegates to the last reunion of Civil War Veterans, Turner Hall, and his escort James H. Milling, entrained for Washington, D.C., to "see the sights."

Mrs. Milling received a telegram from her husband Tuesday stating that they were in Washington and would probably arrive home Friday.

Like the other delegates they report that they are having the time of their lives. Meanwhile, trains pull out of Gettysburg carrying the veterans to their homes in all parts of the United States.

Departing for his St. Louis home, John M. Claypool, 92-year-old commander of the Confederate veterans exulted: "I've just been tickled to death. I've been to lots of reunions, but never anything like this. I knew it would be good, but it turned out better than anything I could have conceive. Claypool and Dr. Overton H. Mennett, G.A.R. commander, declared they have had the "time of their lives." About a 1000 veterans, half of those at the reunion, left for the west on the first two trains. The remainder start tomorrow.

Gettysburg folk, who enjoyed the veterans' visit perhaps more than hundred of thousands of sightseers, gathered at two branch line railroad depots to wave a last good-by.

Twenty-five veterans remained in the army camp hospital and nine others were being treated in hospitals in Gettysburg and nearby Carlisle. Most of the men needed rest but one, John W. Cooper, 91 of Largo, Fla., was reported in critical condition from a heart attack. Most of the others would leave tomorrow, said Lieut. Col Paul D. Hawley of the army medical corps." (July 6, 1938 *Hugo Daily News*, Oklahoma Historical Society)

"A Real Pioneer"

" Pictured above is Uncle Turner Hall, colored Civil War veteran, who will soon celebrate his 101st birthday. He will be given a prominent place in the Thursday evening parade and the Cavalcade 1941 shows. During the Civil War, Uncle Turner was an orderly for Robert E. Lee. He has received many honors because of his age and prominence and even appeared on the NBC program, "We, the People" in New York City. The white and colored citizens of Hugo both designate Uncle Turner as their most distinguished citizen." (*Hugo Daily News*, August 28, 1941, Oklahoma Historical Society)

Out of all the articles, there was one that I received by total surprise. This particular article celebrating Turner, Jr.'s hundredth birthday would be the one that brought me to nothing less than an exuberant dance and to tears before my family. I told my daughter to tell her children and her grandchildren the day she saw her daddy dance over the news that he received about his great-great-grandfather. It was Monday, July 20, 2015, in the midst of the turmoil over the Confederate flag following the aftermath of the nine Black Americans killed in an historic church in South Carolina. On this day, I received a final piece of the puzzle of my ancestor's involvement in the Civil War. There were two important components missing about his story. The first, could his claims be verified? I had a third-party written account of his report serving as an orderly for Robert E. Lee in the August 28, 1941 news article (*The Hugo Daily News*). There was also mention in the November 25, 1937 article (*The Daily Oklahoman*) that he saw General Lee "lots of times." But, of course, I had no way of verifying any claims of his service to the Southern General. I had no reason to doubt but, boy, wouldn't it be sweet to actually be able to say for certain that, indeed, it is true!

I was beyond the point of doubting that he was a Confederate. That much was clear. At this point, it was all about historical accuracy to the best of my ability. I had written the Oklahoma Historical Society to request a second copy of the original articles that I had received in April of 2015. I had also obtained his date of birth and inquired about another article that I knew existed but hadn't been delivered in the first search request. It was an article titled "Turner Hall Has Birthday Today, He's 98 Years Old." The article was in the family possession but it was so faded that we could barely read it. In fact, we had to use a magnifying glass to make out the top half of the article and it was almost impossible to read the bottom portion. I knew I needed to get as much information as possible while the getting was good. So, I requested a specific search of this article. This is one of my favorite articles on Turner, Jr.

"Turner Hall Has Birthday Today. He's 98 Years Old."

"Turner Hall, one of the few surviving Confederate veterans, awoke this morning to find himself 98 years old. When the dawn broke this morning, it was the 35,468th time that daylight had found him still numbered among the living although he went through one of the hardest fought wars in the history of the world.

The venerable colored man, known to almost everybody in Hugo and surround towns, does not show his 98 years. In action and appearance he would be taken for a man of 70. He still has a quick eye, a spry step and continues to get around without assistance. He knows on sight almost everyone he meets on the streets.

Last spring, Hall was awarded a trip with all expenses paid to the last meeting of the Blue and the Gray at Gettysburg. Newsreel cameramen singled him out as a typical example of the colored Confederate soldier and depicted him proudly displaying his medals.

Hall was an orderly for General Robert E. Lee in the Civil War." (*The Hugo Daily News*, October 11, 1938, Oklahoma Historical Society)

This was the third article that we had that made reference to General Robert E. Lee. But this was not the article of surprise that settled my heart and mind on my connection to the Confederacy once and for all. Not only did I receive the ninety-eighth birthday article, a new article emerged during the search since we had narrowed his birthday down to October 11. His hundredth-year birthday celebration made the news in 1940. A familiar large hat with the title, "Has Birthday," and a subtitle, "Turner Hall," helped me put to rest once and for all that I was as much a son of the Confederacy than any Southerner could claim. In fact, one historical aspect in this article settled a personal secret suspicion that I have carried for years. I remembered the words that I read in the book, *Black Confederates*, in Otis Hayes, Jr's account of his conversations with Turner, Jr., in relationship to General Lee as being "unverified." So, for some time, I have been trying to, at a minimum, verify what roles an orderly played in the Civil War. That would be the extent that I would know my ancestor's journey in the war. In fact, this has led me to studying the Civil War with a slave's perspective in mind. Anything that I can find about the Civil War that has accounts of slaves and their role and disposition during the war is of great interest to me.

I had resolved to put the idea of attempting to verify any claims of my great-great-grandfather out of my mind. It would literally be like trying to find a needle in a haystack. Think about it. How can I verify something that wasn't verifiable? A hundred and fifty years later, how in the world am I to verify any claim that a former slave made when I knew very well that most involvement of slaves in the Civil War were not recorded? It was a helpless plea to say the least. So, you can image my excitement and the reason I danced with joy when I came to the last sentence of this newly discovered article celebrating his hundredth birthday: "His claims to this distinction have been verified from records in the war department." (*The Hugo Daily News*, October 13, 1940, Oklahoma Historical Society)

Any Civil War student will know the significance of this sentence. Point being, verification is everything to those who study the Civil War. The history making of the Civil War, in my opinion, makes it the supreme historical event of our country. However, I can't explain to you the frustration it has been to know that your ancestor has claims to history that you know deep down you will never be able to verify. Well, I no longer have that burden. I don't have to verify his claims. Someone else has already done that and that is good enough for me. After all, the accuracy of verification in his day would perhaps be more certain of any accuracy that I could lay down now. But this wasn't my secret suspicion at all. As stated previously, I didn't doubt his claims, because men were truthful men in those days.

There was more. As a student of the Civil War, I have read the accounts many times and often came across references to orderlie's performing their duty. Commonly, no mention of name or even race is given in these accounts. Just "orderly." I'm also aware that an orderly was not necessarily Black; many Whites served in this capacity, and some with greater distinction than others. I could imagine that Robert E. Lee would have had many official military orderlies during the course of the war. So, I had to be careful in my understanding of my ancestor's role as an orderly and how and where he may have been used in various capacities for several individuals.

I did have one verbal witness from Otis Hayes, Jr. to the claim that Turner, Jr. had taken care of Traveller, General Robert E. Lee's horse. (By the way, the first horse owned by my son was named Traveller in honor of his great great-great-grandfather. And this was well before we knew any connection that he had actually claimed to have taken care of one of the most famous war horses of all times.) I could only imagine that an orderly's duty would have been to take care of the horses so that's the hope that I had when my son was fifteen years old and we bought that horse for his birthday in 2009. Moreover, there is a Civil War account that I have read numerous times and wondered if it was remotely possible that my great-great-grandfather could have been there to witness an illustrious Civil War scene. It was at the surrender of General Robert E. Lee to General Grant at Appomattox Courthouse in Virginia on April 9, 1865. The account reads as following:

> "At a little before 4 o'clock General Lee shook hands with General Grant, bowed to the other officers, and with Colonel Marshall left the room. One after another we followed, and passed out to the porch. Lee signaled to his orderly to bring up his horse, and while the animal was being bridled the

general stood on the lowest step and gazed sadly in the direction of the valley beyond where his army lay—now an army of prisoners. He smote his hands together a number of times in an absent sort of way; seemed not to see the group of Union officers in the yard who rose respectfully at his approach, and appeared unconscious of everything about him. All appreciated the sadness that overwhelmed him, and he had the personal sympathy of every one who beheld him at this supreme moment of trial. The approach of his horse seemed to recall him from his reverie, and he at once mounted. General Grant now stepped down from the porch, and, moving toward him, saluted him by raising his hat. He was followed in this act of courtesy by all our officer present: Lee raised his hat respectfully, and rode off to break the sad news to the brave fellows whom he had so long commanded." ("Surrender at Appomattox, 1865," EyeWitness to History, www.eyewitnesstohistory.com, 1997)

What a scene. To be an eye witness to this account must have been breathtaking. I have read this account many times wondering about that orderly. I have held a crazy secret suspicion that perhaps it was my great-great-grandfather. I am almost certain based upon historical records that this orderly was not my ancestor. But to have that thought has been a stimulating aspect of my research.

Yet, hold on. That hundredth birthday article says records in the war department have verified his claims. What claims?

Well, the article lays out several claims. One is that he was in the Southern army. I knew that already. The second claim is that he was an orderly for Robert E. Lee. I knew about that claim as well. However, it was a new claim that causes me to tremble every time I read it. He was at the surrender of Lee to Grant at Appomattox. Now, that was a shocker. I don't claim he was the orderly that brought Traveller to the general on that day. That orderly was Sergeant Tucker. Tucker was one of the general's official military orderlies. I don't claim that my ancestor was an official military orderly as designated by the Southern army. I think my ancestor picked that distinction up throughout the course of the war as he performed routine servant duties for the general when in his presence upon numerous occasions. However, I do believe he was there to witness the surrender of the Southern army at Appomattox. There is one more account of orderly servants being at Appomattox. I am inclined to believe that one of these men would have been Turner Hall, Jr. At Appomattox the Confederates received over 28,000 parole passes. It is recorded that at least thirty-six of these passes were for Blacks. These men were the servants, cooks, and slaves present in various capacities according to the Southern Historical Society Papers. Some of these men are named as teamsters and at least sixteen of them were not named. Again, I don't contend that Turner Hall was a Black Confederate soldier. He was a servant in the Confederate army, and a proud one indeed. He cherished his memories of his time in the war and held dear his association with General Robert E. Lee and Nathan Bedford Forrest. As his great-great-grandson, that's enough for me. Black men took on various roles in the war just as White men did. His service was of no less value in the cause of war and thus must be honored as such. The dilemma of war records creates a problem for Blacks who desire to know the role that their ancestors played in the Southern army, and it presents a current-day problem for the average Confederate ancestor who is aware that slaves were by their ancestors' side. Here is the problem. The record shows that 36 slaves received parole on behalf of the Confederate army of Northern Virginia. However, just because we only have record of 36, it doesn't mean that only 36 were there. What we need to embrace as African Americans is the fact that we were on the scene. Many of my dear, hard-core Confederates will ask proof of every single detail in the Civil War without ever mentioning the fact that most of the Confederate records burned when the Rebels fled the capitol of Richmond, Virginia. Even had these records been preserved, however, they would be spotty, at best, regarding the history of the Negro. We don't know the full detail of the role Blacks played in the war because we don't have all the records and what was written after the war was almost always a discredit to the Negroes service on both sides. So, those who hold on to Confederate heritage want African Americans to be proud of their ancestors who participated in this heritage without given allowance of what history has done to destroy those connections. As a result, there is often little defense or proof with which to overwhelm African Americans as to their Confederate connections. Well, I have found my heritage, and I am proud of it. Not one hard-core Confederate or Black nationalist will change the fact that my ancestor played a role in the making of this great country:

> "Uncle Turner is a Civil War veteran, having served in the Southern army and was orderly for General Robert E. Lee commander of the Southern armies and was present when Gen. Lee surrendered to General Grant. His memory is excellent and he enjoys relating his experience in connection with his services for the famous Southern general." (*Hugo Daily News*, Oct. 13, 1940, Oklahoma Historical Society).

What started for me in 2008 at a family reunion has climaxed in the middle of the debate on the Confederate flag in 2015. Tears come to my eyes as I realize that my research into my family history has not been in vain. To know that my great-great-grandfather was present at Appomattox at the end of the beginning of a new era for slaves is a humbling fact. That he lived through the war to tell about his story and to lay claims to his Confederate heritage is mindblowing to me. To be able to write about his story and my journey is an honor. I am intimately tied to the history of our country, the Civil War, and the existing tension between those who struggle to see the Confederate flag remain versus those who struggle to see it come down. I am connected to two of the greatest military generals of all times, Robert E. Lee and Nathan Bedford Forrest, in a strange and twisted way, but in a way that is historic and unique. It would be enough to be connected to one of these great generals. I am connected to two great Confederate generals through Turner Hall, Jr. This gives me the reason to say that I am a two-time Confederate over. That's Southern slang to mean I am twice as much a Confederate than any other man. I just happen to be Black.

I am fortunate to be able to write about my great-great-grandfather's story. I realize that he was not the only Black slave who served in the Confederacy. Some even fought as soldiers. Opening up one family history with research will lead you down bifurcated roads that have twists and turns that are often unexpected. This is one journey that I am glad I decided to take.

I will forever cherish this story and the role my ancestor played in the Civil War. I pray that it is never forgotten. Unfortunately, because of the brutal injustice imposed upon African Americans by post-Civil War writers, many African Americans can't make any connections to the Civil War. Their connections were destroyed, ignored, hidden, or portrayed with malice. As a result, the heroism of slave Robert Smalls of South Carolina and freeman of color named William Tillman are virtually unknown by African Americans today. Before I share with you the heroism of these two Blacks, let me share a few official military records of some of the service our people conducted in the war in the Confederate army.

"Pickets were thrown out that night, and Captain Hennessy, Company E, of the Ninth Connecticut, having been sent out with his company, captured a colored rebel scout, well mounted, who had been sent out to watch our movements." Federal Official Records, Series I, Vol. XLIX, Part II, pg. 253 - April 6, 1865:

"The rebels [Forrest] are recruiting negro troops at Enterprise, Miss., and the negroes are all enrolled in the State." Federal Official Records, Series I, Vol. XIV, pg. 24, second paragraph - "It is also difficult to state the force of the enemy, but it could not have been less than from 600 to 800. There were six companies of mounted riflemen, besides infantry, among which were a considerable number of colored men." referring to Confederate forces opposing him at Pocotaligo, SC., Colonel B. C. Christ, 50th Pennsylvania Volunteer Infantry, official report of May 30, 1862

"Seventy free blacks enlisted in the Confederate Army in Lynchburg, Virginia. Sixteen companies of free men of color marched through Augusta, Georgia on their way to fight in Virginia.

"Negroes in the Confederate Army," Journal of Negro History, Charles Wesle, Vol. 4, #3, [1919,] 244-245 -

"I can assure you [Father,] of a certainty, that the rebels have negro soldiers in their army. One of their best sharp shooters, and the boldest of them all here is a negro. He dug himself a rifle pit last night [16 April 1863] just across the river and has been annoying our pickets opposite him very much to-day. You can see him plain enough with the naked eye, occasionally, to make sure that he is a "wooly-head," and with a spy-glass there is no mistaking him." (From James G. Bates' letter to his father reprinted in the 1 May 1863 "Winchester [Indiana] Journal" [the 13th IVI ["Hoosier Regiment"] was involved in operations around the Suffolk, Virginia area in April-May 1863])

To find out what was going on with Blacks during the war, I found it most helpful to find out what Black writers were saying before and during the war. I will refer to the story of Robert Smalls and William Tillman, if nothing more than to stir up a need for African Americans to discover the richness of African-American history that is tied to the Civil War. For those that are not content that my ancestor's role was not as stimulating to them as they would prefer, and because as one of my first cousins said to me at the family reunion, "that's the one who fought on the wrong side?" (I looked at him and said, "That's the one who fought and served!"), I contend that any role in war is a significant role. I think any role in the Civil War has even more special meaning to the establishment of this great nation. But let's look at these two men who surpassed anything that any Union soldier ever accomplished on the high seas of war.

The Story of Robert Smalls, *U.S. Steamship Augusta*, Off Charleston, May 13, 1862:

"Sir, I have the honor to inform you that the rebel-armed gunboat *Planter* was brought out to us this morning from Charleston by eight contrabands (slaves) and delivered up to the squadron. Five colored women and three children are also on board. She was the armed dispatch and transportation steamer attached to the engineer department at Charleston, under Brig.-Gen. Ripley. At four in the morning, in the absence of the captain who was on shore, she left her wharf close to the government office and headquarters, with the Palmetto and Confederate flags flying, and passed the successive forts, saluting as usual, by blowing the steam-whistle. After getting beyond the range of the last gun, they hauled down the rebel flags, and hoisted a white one. *The Onward* was the inside ship of the blockading squadron in the main channel, and was preparing to fire when her commander made out the white flag.

"The armament of the steamer is a thirty-two pounder, on pivot, and a fine twenty-four pound howitzer. She has, besides, on her deck, four other guns, one seven-inch, rifled, which were to be taken on the following morning to a new fort on the middle ground. One of the four belonged to Fort Sumter, and had been struck, in the rebel attack, on the muzzle. Robert Small, the intelligent slave, and pilot of the boat, who performed this bold feat so skillfully, is a superior man to any who have come into our lines, intelligent as any of them have been. His information has been most interesting, and portions of it of the utmost importance. The steamer is quite a valuable acquisition to the squadron by her good machinery and very light draught. The bringing out of this steamer would have done credit to anyone. I do not know whether, in the view of the Government, the vessel will be considered a prize; but if so, I respectfully submit to the Department the claims of the man Small and his associates. Very respectfully, your obedient servant, S. F. DuPont, "Flag-Officer Commanding."

Commercial Advertiser said:

> "We are forced to confess that this is a heroic act, and that the Negroes deserve great praise. Small is a middle-aged Negro, and his features betray nothing of the firmness of character he displayed. He is said to be one of the most skillful pilots of Charleston, and to have a thorough knowledge of all the ports and inlets of South Carolina." (William Wells Brown, *The Negro in The American Rebellion*, 1867)

> "*The Planter* is just such a vessel as is needed to navigate the shallow waters between Hilton Head and the adjacent islands, and will prove almost invaluable to the Government. It is proposed, I hear, by the commodore, to recommend the appropriation of $20,000.00 as a reward to the plucky Africans who have distinguished themselves by this gallant service, $5,000 to be given to the

pilot, and the remainder to be divided among his companions. (William Wells Brown, *The Negro in The American Rebellion*,1867)

The Story of William Tillman:

"In the month of June, 1861, the schooner *S. J. Waring*, from New York, bound to South America, was captured on the passage by the rebel privateer *Jeff Davis*, a prize crew put on board, consisting of a captain, mate and four seamen; and the vessel set sail for the port of Charleston, SC. Three of the original crew was retained on board, a German as steersman, a Yankee who was put in irons, and a black man named William Tillman, the steward and cook of the schooner. The latter was put to work at his usual business and told that he was henceforth the property of the Confederate States, and would be sold, on his arrival at Charleston, as a slave. Night comes on; darkness covers the sea, the vessel is gladdening swiftly toward the South; the rebels, one after another, retire to their berths; the hour of midnight approaches; all is silent in the cabin; the captain is asleep; the mate, who has charge of the watch, takes his brandy toddy, and reclines upon the quarter-deck. The Negro thinks of home and all its endearments; he sees in the dim future chains and slavery.

He resolves, and determines to put the resolution into practice upon the instant. Armed with a heavy club, he proceeds to the captain's room. He strikes the fatal blow: he feels the pulse, and all is still. He next goes to the adjoining room: another blow is struck, and the black man is master of the cabin. Cautiously he ascends to the deck, strikes the mate: the officer is wounded but not killed. He draws his revolver, and calls for help. The crew are aroused: they are hastening to aid their commander. The Negro repeats his blows with the heavy club: the rebel falls dead at Tillman's feet. The African seizes the revolver, drives the crew below deck, orders the release of the Yankee, puts the enemy in irons, and proclaims himself master of the vessel. *The Waring's* head is turned toward New York, with the stars and stripes flying, a fair wind, and she rapidly retraces her steps. A storm comes up: more men are needed to work the ship. Tillman orders the rebels to be unchained and brought on deck. The command is obeyed; and they are put to work, but informed, that, if they show any disobedience, they will be shot down. Five days more, and the *The S. J. Waring* arrives in the port of New York, under the command of William Tillman, the Negro patriot."

The *New York Tribune* said of this event:

"To this colored man was the nation indebted for the first vindication of its honor on the sea." The Federal Government awarded to Tillman the sum of six thousand dollars as prize-money for the capture of the schooner. (William Wells Brown*, The Negro in The American Rebellion*, 1867)

Here are the stories of three brave Black Civil War-era men. They had no formal education, no right to vote, no opportunity for advancement, no right to military service. These were mere men who were faced with obstacles beyond imagination for the average African-American man today.

Two were slaves and one was free in a country that had condoned slavery for four hundred years. They all survived, though, through very different means. My ancestor used chivalry and service as a slave. The other man overcame with ingenuity and intelligence. Finally, one overcame with a club and a revolver. One man fought and served under the Confederate flag. Two men fought under the American flag. Which flag represented a system of oppression and slavery from the perspective of the African ?

We forget that slavery existed over three hundred and ninty-six years under the American flag. The Confederate flag came during the last four years of slavery. The greatest tragedy is that as African Americans we don't know these stories. And yet, we disown the men of this era as if they were mere pawns in a game of chess. These men fought, served, and lived during a time that was the beginning of a new formation for our country. They were more than pioneers. As much as I want to say that they were the foundations in which African-American men are built upon today, I am too embarrassed to say that. It appears that they are more like capstones or the apex of what it means to be African-American men. I say this because, if these men had the odds that the average African-American male had today, they would walk among us as giants. Why? It is because these men and women overcame unbelievable obstacles. They could not read or write but they could navigate ships on the high seas, they could command ships and navigate waters. They were slaves, but they weren't afraid to master the trade of their day in order to accomplish great heights. They could traverse land or sea, and discharge their duties with complete competence.

This is why I write of the need for Black guilt instead of White guilt. When I think of men like these, I hang my head every time I see a young Black man arrested for senseless acts of violence and crime that plague our communities; when I witness the degradation of the Black family into a cycle of poverty because men will not take their rightful place as men and be respectful citizens of our society and raise their children to be respectful citizens in a free country. Martin Luther King, Jr., said, "Freedom has always been expensive." Why are so many of our men incarcerated? Too few seek to serve our country through military service when opportunities are enormous before them. On the eve of the emancipation proclamation in 1863, slave George Payne explained freedom this way:

> "Let me tell you, though, don't be too free! De lazy man can't go to heaven. You must be honest, an' work, an' show dat you is fit to be free; an' de lord

will bless you an' Abrum Lincum. Amen!" (George Payne, Slave 1863, William Wells Brown, *The Negro in The American Rebellion*)

Turner Hall was a hard worker. He didn't just work for the Walton family for five generations. When he arrived in Oklahoma, the first thing he did was help the Waltons build their family home. He then built his own personal cabin behind their home and it became a "landmark for many years." He was a janitor for the First Baptist church for fifteen years. He was janitor of the Ross building for thirteen years and the First Presbyterian Church for nearly ten years. If there is any man in our family who does not work, we will be the first to say, he doesn't deserve to eat. That doesn't mean we don't feed the hungry or the poor. It simply means we place a very high value on hard work. There was never a day that a stranger couldn't get a meal at my grandmother's home. She cooked for her family and always prepared enough for the straggler that would come to her house with her grandchildren or her kids. The descendants of Turner Hall, Jr. are hard workers. My dad and his siblings, to this day, are very hard workers. They made their living by the sweat of their brow. They worked their way up from the bottom of manufacturing, military service, and education to the top of the workforce. They have all done well by the grace of God and by working hard and demonstrating their ability to be dependable workers.

My dad was plant manager for Mid-South Packing Company in Tupelo. I remember seeing him get off work when I was a young man. All supervisors wore white hats on his job. His hat was red. The buck stopped with him. I was always proud of him knowing that he was at the top of his industry without a formal education.

Uncle Willie retired from manufacturing and started his own manufacturing company. He was very successful and retired a second time from his work.

Currently, my brother, Kenny Hill, is the owner and operator of this company, with my dad right by his side. Uncle Willie still has one eye on everything that goes on.

Aunt Pearl retired in education as an administrator and school principal in Michigan schools, being the only college graduate (Michigan State, Administration) in the family.

Aunt Avis is the manager of Alan White's Furniture in Shannon, Mississippi.

Uncle Ralph retired from the Air Force and continues to work in his industry as an expert in aviation mechanics.

Uncle Earnest, a Vietnam Veteran, retired as a plant manager from manufacturing in Grand Rapids, Michigan.

Uncle Herbert, a laborer, was the president of the Union Association for Eljer's Manufacturing in Tupelo and traveled throughout the United States and Canada on his job.

They all got their hard work ethics from their parents who got it from their parents, who got it from their parents. One of my grandfather's favorite saying was, "If you are going to be a ditch digger, be the best ditch digger you can be." Ras Arnold was an uneducated man who learned to master electrical work and plumbing.

My grandmother, Arine Arnold, was "The Help" for the prominent Black family (owners of Black's Clothing Store) in Nettleton. To say that "Moma Arine" and Mrs. Black were anything short of best friends for life would be an understatement. These two friends were inseparable in life. They are truly no longer separated by race, class, or which side of town they lived own. They are now united as one in the same heaven that awaits all who put their trust in Christ. Just like her grandfather, Turner Hall, Jr., who found a friend and brother in Nathan Bedford Forrest, their friendship was built upon a relationship that spanned over forty years. I'm certain that relationship had its ups and downs. But they persevered accepting the same Christ as their Redeemer.

It saddens me today as I see the numerous and unlimited opportunities for educational experiences that are never tapped into because far too many of our young men and women want an easy way to success. Hard work is no longer the way for too many.

AM I MY BROTHER'S KEEPER?

Now Cain said to his brother Abel, "Let's go out to the field."

While they were in the field, Cain attacked his brother Abel and killed him. Then the LORD said to Cain, "Where is your brother Abel?"

"I don't know," he replied. "Am I my brother's keeper?"

The LORD said, "What have you done? Listen! Your brother's blood cries out to me from the ground." (Gen. 4:8–10)

A modern version of the "Am I my brother's keeper?" question came as a result of the 1992 Rodney King riots in Los Angeles. At a post-riot news conference, King coined the question of my generation when he asked, "Can't we all just get along?"

I have come to understand, in very meaningful ways, that without Christ, it is impossible to do two things. First, it is impossible to be your brother's keeper. It doesn't matter if he is White or Black. Secondly, it is impossible for all of us to get along. Humanity is broken. That brokenness shows up in our hatred of one another, our bitterness toward each other, and our unforgiving spirits toward one another. Unfortunately the answer to both questions is a resounding NO! We live in a society where we are NOT our brothers' keepers. I want to answer the question emphatically, absolutely not. We can't just all get along! There will always be something that comes up to remind us of our past and provide splinters to wounds. Unless you have reconciled your past and/or your wounds through the blood of Christ, you are doomed to a life of bitterness, unforgiveness, and hatred.

Being that I am African American, let me share with you how this is too often displayed in our communities. When I was in physical therapy school, I rented an apartment from a very successful African-American lawyer in Jackson. He would visit the apartment routinely to monitor the upkeep. I had a picture that portrayed a Black arm stretching over a mountain reaching for another Black arm. This art had been a centerpiece of my living area since my days at Jackson State University. It was a defining principle that I lived by. It was a portrait of one brother helping another brother to overcome mountaintops. Well, I wasn't ready for the perspective of my landlord. He introduced me to a concept that I had never heard of. He asked me, "Young man, have up ever heard the story of a crab in a bucket?"

I replied, "No."

Well, most Black Southerners know exactly where this is going. But, let me tell the rest of you one of the hidden painful secrets among Blacks. This is very painful for the most part. Black folk will talk about this among themselves but we don't prefer to air our dirty laundry to other folks. This particular issue is a troublesome one to the soul of the African American. Moreover, we all have our different reasons as to why and how this is our narrative. This issue has deep roots in our communities and this was my introduction to it. However, it would be years later before I would come face to face with the reality of this. Be it known that I rejected every notion of this mentality upon my introduction. I distinctly remember the pride in which this well-known Black professional gave me his thoughts about my art. He smiled as he told me there was something in the picture that I could not see.

I looked again as I had stared at this picture a few times. He then pointed to the picture and said, "As soon as you grab that hand to lift him up he will pull out a razor and cut your wrist as you pull him up." We debated this for over an hour. He left me with theses words, "You keep living and you will find out!"

I never forgot this exchange. It would stay with me throughout the remainder of my time in physical therapy school.

I graduated from the Physical Therapy school at the University of Mississippi in 1991. One year after graduation, I began my mountaintop reaching experience. I volunteered once a month at Jackson State University, mentoring college students as they pursued their goal to become a physical therapist. After the second year, I added Tougaloo College. For four years, I reached over the mountain to pull others up over the hills. At the end of the four years I started to see a trend that caused me to redirect my energy. First, I saw a rapid decline in the students' desire to succeed. More and more students were farther and farther down the mountain. They were harder to reach because they had not adequately prepared themselves. They were showing up at the foot of the mountain too late and without the tools necessary for the climb. Secondly, I noticed a trend of former mountain climbers turning their hand away from those that were seeking their help. Those that had succeeded would do little if nothing to help others climb. Frequently, I would receive calls from former students giving me information on some poor student who was a family member or son of a friend that needed help to climb the mountain of becoming a physical therapist. It became clear to me that everyone would not reach back. These were therapists who were now employed with great incomes but were passing students off as if they had the plague.

This was just the beginning of my crab bucket experience. I had not been cut yet but the bucket would soon be full as I started my own private practice in a predominately African-American city. Moreover, a very highly skilled Black professional community existed. Ten years later, I wanted to go back and shake the hand of my former landlord. Unfortunately, he had suddenly died and I was never able to tell him that I had come to experience and know the pain of being in the bucket with a lot of crabs. Brutal is an understatement. All the years of preparation to combat the enemy, and the enemy wasn't who I thought he was. I found out that my biggest enemy looked just like me. He certainly wasn't a blue-eyed devil. In fact, when I sold my company, the blue-eyed physician was my biggest referral source and had it not been for him I wouldn't have been able to feed my family. I received referrals from many White physicians that I never laid eyes on. On the other hand, the unbelievable life experience of working with African Americans was eye opening to say the least.

MY CRAB EXPERIENCES

THE GREEDY DOCTOR

I owned the first Black independent physical therapy clinic in the capitol city. Jackson is a Black professional haven, if you will. A large majority of Mississippi's Black professionals practice in the Jackson metropolitan area. When I was in physical therapy school at the University of Mississippi, I served as the vice president of the Minority Student Affairs club. The president of the organization was a medical student that shared a similar story as mine. Most, if not all of us, in the group were first generational college students or from impoverished upbringings.

After graduation, I developed a professional relationship with this physician. She referred patients and I provided care accordingly. About two years into the relationship, her referrals stopped. I visited her after I discovered she had started doing physical therapy in a non-conventional way for her patients. I strongly suggested to her that this was not a viable solution for her patients and for her well-being. She had been introduced to a concept of referring patients to herself. Sadly, several years after she refused to listen to the direct ethical challenges of doing what was right and good for the well-being of her patients (overwhelmingly Black), she faced over a hundred years of incarceration for Medicare fraud. Sadly, a common theme in the African-American community was, "They doing it to her because she is Black." However, records in court showed she had billed millions of dollars. No, it wasn't because she was Black. It was because she was stealing. There was no reason for me to wonder why she stopped referring patients to me. She received a multi-year prison sentence.

The Hit Man from Chicago

This crab experience is perhaps the funniest of all them but it happened. I had two offices at the time. I owned one in Jackson and one in a little small town outside of the Jackson metro area. There was a group of Black physicians who operated a clinic and provided referrals for physical therapy to my clinic. I received a call to set up a meeting with one of the physicians whose practice did not warrant any referrals to my office. I thought the request was strange but it was granted since he did not refer patients to me. Upon arrival to my office, I noticed the physician was not alone. He had with him an African-American gentleman of great stature. He must have been six foot three inches, with very broad shoulders. He was wearing a pinstripe suit with snakeskin shoes. Church ground clean. This brother was sharp. The physician introduced him as their new office manager that would oversee all out-sourced referrals. He stated to my partner and me, "I understand that we send you over 90 percent of your referrals and if you guys don't come in under us, we are going to pull the plug on you. We are going to go in-house with everything."

Wow! This guy didn't have a gun to my head but I had watched enough movies to know a shake down when I saw one. But the fact that he had the pinstripe suit and the snakeskin shoes made it all surreal to me. I was looking at a real live mobster type figure attempting to shake me down as if I was some punk on the street. And the white-coat bosses that sent this guy were Black guys who I had worked with for years in a small community with a large African-American population. A community that was instrumental in the civil rights era. This group hired a White therapist to work in their office. Within six months, the therapist had resigned and that was the end of their attempt to "go inhouse." I never got another referral from them.

THE NAACP FRONT

One of the first invitations I got in the local community was one from the local NAACP president who was also a physician. He was a pioneer in the community in some regards. Blacks marched to secure hospital privileges for this physician back in the '60s. Proverbs 27:6 is one of my favorites and it helped me tremendously in this instance. It reads, "the wound of a friend can be trusted but an enemy multiplies kisses."

I remember the day I saw it coming as clearly as if it was this day. The physician's office manager came to my office to "visit your facilities." With a smile as big as Chester the cat himself, she proceeded to walk the building to inspect all of my equipment. I then realized that this guy had sent a spy to my office to see what he needed to provide physical therapy in his office. At that moment, I began to show her everything that I had and how it worked. After all, if they were going to take care of my people, I wanted them to know what they needed. The entire time this lady was smiling and telling how much they appreciated me taking care of their patients. Yet, I could feel her deceit. It was so thick I could cut a cake with it. They hired a White therapist and stopped referring business to me the following week. The therapist resigned after three months and that was the end of that. I never got another referral from my NAACP friend.

The Black Hospital

A small hospital in rural Mississippi was in need of physical therapy services. An all-Black board, a Black CEO, and a Black CFO governed this particular hospital. For two years we courted the CEO and CFO to allow us to establish a contract with the hospital to provide services to the community. After failed attempts to convince them of this direction we decided to open a freestanding clinic in the community. At the direction of the primary Black physician in the community we gave one last attempt to secure a contract with the hospital prior to proceeding with the freestanding clinic. Another two weeks expired and the administrator finally agreed to present our contract after two years and two weeks. The boards' attorney was a White guy whose wife was a physical therapist. Need I say more? She got the contract in two weeks and that was that. When I pushed the CFO to explain their decision, her answer was this, "Well, we have a Black board and if we present anything to them that's Black, they will not approve it." Ouch!

The Largest Crab Emerges

During the election of our first Black president, Barack Obama, we witnessed this crab experience on a national level.

When most African Americans were elated at the possibility of electing the first African-American president, we witnessed a most embarrassing but all-to-familiar problem. An unlikely source but not surprising was the old crab claw given by none other than the Rev. Jessie Jackson when he desired to have Barrack Obama castrated for "talking down to Black folks," as he put it. At that time, I realized again that my former landlord had shared something with me that I would never understand but would often see throughout my adult experiences. It's one thing to disagree with a man but to desire him castrated is to signify your desire to see him destroyed.

As an African-American male, one of the biggest disappointments that I have had over the past eight years in the Obama administration is to witness the failure as a community to stop violent crimes among young African-American men. Notice, I did not say, "Obama's failure." However, you would think with the election of our first African-American president, the young African-American males would be inspired to greatness, instead of violence. Let me be clear, the president is not to blame. I have surely felt a lack of outcry from our community in this regard. Where is the marching and protests over the thousand lives claimed in Chicago from January to June 2015? During the same time that Blacks were protesting over the death of Travon Martin, Eric Garner, Michael Brown, and

Freddie Grey, thousands of African-American men were being slaughtered at the hands of other African Americans.

This is not to diminish the spotlight on what African Americans perceive as injustice in the criminal justice system. As Christians, we all are to fight injustice. This is simply to cast a broader light on a much larger problem and the lack of response from the African-American community. Where is the national outcry?

Many have attempted to curtail the violence. But I'm not talking about curtailing it or slowing it down. I'm talking about demanding that it stop with just as much passion as we demand justice for those killed by injustice. Let's attack Black homicides and the senseless crimes in our communities like we attack the Confederate flag and the cases of injustice that we are quickly to rally support for.

Where are the loudmouth preachers, politicians, and movie stars when our communities and heritage are being betrayed by savage acts of violence and hatred toward one another? We have communities that suffer from chronic failure to uphold common decency for our elders, respect for our women, and wholesale disregard for the welfare of children. How long will it take to realize that White folks today or one hundred and fifty years ago are not our problem? We are our worst enemy. We are not our brother's keeper and it is showing up everywhere in our communities.

If our young men are not dying in the streets like dogs they are being locked up in prisons herded like cattle. In fact, dogs and cattle have more respect in society than the average Black male, thus the movement, Black Lives Matter. If Black lives matter, why are we wholesale murdering each other in the streets? I'll tell you why. Because we want Black lives to matter only when we want them to matter. This ought not be. But we have allowed it. Young men are fathering multiple children by different women, condemning multiple generations to poverty. And what do we say? We parade these facts through lyrics in our most popular songs. "It's just my baby daddy!"

Moreover, thousands upon thousands fail to seize the opportunity to be educated and therefore are not useful for the workforce and not prepared for military service. I see this daily in my line of work as a home health physical therapist. I see first-hand the degradation of the family and the impact that it's having on our people. Hopelessness and despair due to lack of education, lack of skills, poor work ethics, and lack of faith runs through our communities like a plague. Crime is high, abortion rates are skyrocketing, military readiness is down. The productivity of young African-American males is staggeringly low.

In the backdrop of all of this many of us want White folks to feel guilty for the crimes of their ancestors and the existing hatred of a few toward Black folks. Even if there is a reason to be guilty, and I contend it no longer exists, the biggest guilt should be on our shoulders. What we need NOW is Black guilt, not White guilt!

After all, it was our people who endured slavery, endured post-Civil War time, and endured the Civil Rights era. It was our people who died, sacrificed, and worked like dogs that we may have a better future. It was our people who sacrificed that one day we could see a brother be elected as president of the United States of America. One of my favorite Martin Luther King, Jr., quotes is, "Freedom has always been an expensive thing." At the expense of four million slaves and at the expense of generations of suffering and sacrifice, we squander opportunities, waste talent, and fail to cultivate family, faith, and respect. We won't even go vote. It took us over a hundred years of persecution to earn the freedom to vote.

It is clear to me that slavery was to this day the greatest failure of the implied command to be our brother's keeper. I think the second greatest failure is the holocaust that killed millions of Jews. What makes slavery worse is that it was an institution that occurred over a four hundred-year period of time. What's even more mind boggling about this greatest offense of the implied law of God to be our brother's keeper is that it was other Africans selling their brothers into slavery. Moreover, you can also find records of free Africans in America who owned slaves themselves. A prominent African American in

Vicksburg, Mississippi, Robert Johnson, owned twelve slaves at the time of his death. He even had slave quarters behind his home, which can still be viewed as a national registered landmark.

However, I think the biggest violation of the "brother's keeper" concept is among African-American males who commit wholesale homicide and perpetuate fatherless children in our communities. Slavery, race, racism, being African American, civil rights, White heritage, and a post-racial America are all complex things. They are not black and white, as many of us want them to be. The Rodney King riots in Los Angeles, California, brought forth the same question that Cain asked God. King asked the question of the decade, if not the century, "Can't we all just get along?" Again, the answer to that question is a resounding NO! I believe mankind is incapable of this great moral challenge without the intervention of a great moral Guide. Hatred has been in our hearts from the point of original sin until this day. Cain's killing of his brother Abel was indeed the first act of racial discrimination, bias, profiling, murder, jealousy, strife, contention, and blame. We are humanly incapable of getting along. Mankind and his strife has occurred since the beginning of times. It shouldn't be a mystery to us why Cain's question, "Am I my brother's keeper?" is not at the end of the Holy Scriptures but in the beginning.

A primary standard of Christianity starts at what I call "the keeper's point." This is the moment in time that each man succumbs to the interest of others and not just the interest of himself. I don't have to be a keeper of my Confederate brother's culture or heritage but I can learn to value it and honor it as an intricate reality of who I am in Christ. I believe God has helped me understand a fundamental truth of the Gospel. It is this: Those who differ the most from you are the ones you need to love the most. I don't believe it is possible to acquiesce this kind of love without redemption in Christ. This is the reason man is full of hatred, sin, bitterness, and strife. I have a sweet acceptance of who I am and who others are only because of Christ.

Arnold & Elliott Family Rules

Always be honest (Proverbs 12:22)

Count your blessings (Psalms 34:1–3)

Forgive and forget (Micah 7:18)

Be supportive of one another (Acts 20:35)

Be kind and tenderhearted (Ephesians 4:32)

Keep your promises (Romans 4:21)

Comfort one another (1 Thessalonians 4:18)

And above all:

Love one another (Peter 1:22)

In Honor and Dedication to My Ancestors

Great-Great-Grandparents

Turner Hall, Jr. & Francis Dilworth Hall

Lucian "Paw Dick" Arnold & Momma Jossie

Great Grandparents

Bennie Elliott and Mama Will

ABOUT THE AUTHOR
AL ARNOLD

I am a native-born Mississippian. I am African American. I am a Christian. I am a Husband. I am a father of two boys and one girl. I am a Southerner. Thanks to an ancestry.com DNA test, I can be a little more specific. Eighty-four percent of my DNA is from Africa. Fifteen percent of my DNA is from Europe. The remaining one percent is of West Asian descent. My ancestral roots are largely from Nigeria and Scandinavia (Sweden, Norway, and Denmark) with trace roots from West Africa and West Europe. It is estimated that over 3.5 million slaves were from Nigeria during the slave trade. It is estimated that over two million Scandinavians immigrated to America between 1820 and 1920. Somewhere in the beautiful and yet ugly mix of things, my African ancestry mixed with my Viking ancestry and I am who I am today by the Grace of God.

I am a descendent of a proud Black Confederate and a former slave. It is in this Grace that I have come to appreciate all of who I am and all of who others are. If they belong to the family of God through Christ, I am all the more compelled to love them. If they do not belong to the family of God through Christ, I am all the more extremely compelled to love them.

alarnold@orderlyforlee.com
www.orderlyforlee.com
Facebook: orderlyforlee

THE AFRICAN-AMERICAN CHARGE
"TELL IT LIKE IT IS!"

"I have done my duty to uphold the good name of
Turner Hall, Jr. I guard his history with the sword of a
soldier. He is no longer a forgotten Confederate. I seek
to perpetuate his virtues and principles for which he
lived."

The truth is that slaves and free Blacks were intimately
engaged in the Civil War on both sides. They served various
capacities on various fronts. It is a mistake to think that slaves
and free Blacks served without a free spirit and willing heart
within the Confederate army. Their claims have not been
rendered the respect they deserve by history and African
Americans. True history cannot be set forth rightly without the
whole of it. No one is holding up the banner of truth that
represents the Black Confederate and the roles of Blacks in the
Civil War.

Here I stand, a descendent of a slave, writing to tell the
truth about him, and his values, honor, and loyalty to the
Confederate army. After the war, he returned home more of a
Confederate than he was when he left to serve. Thereafter, he
lived as a Confederate and died as a Confederate, never releasing
the battle flag for which he served.

We should strive to see that Blacks of his generation be remembered and held in high esteem for their service. I stand to declare the truth of my journey of my Confederate heritage, living out and bearing witness of who I am as a modern African-American Christian man. I am standing by the grace and knowledge of the ultimate truth claim. Christ will set you free!